The 3 Dimensions of Improving Student Performance

Finding the Right Solutions to the Right Problems

The 3 Dimensions of Improving Student Performance

Finding the Right Solutions to the Right Problems

ROBERT RUEDA

Foreword by P. David Pearson

Teachers College, Columbia University
New York and London

Published by Teachers College Press, 1234 Amsterdam Avenue, New York, NY 10027

Library of Congress Cataloging-in-Publication Data

Rueda, Robert.
   The 3 dimensions of improving student performance : finding the right
   solutions to the right problems / Robert Rueda ; foreword by P. David Pearson.
      p. cm.
   Includes bibliographical references and index.
   ISBN 978-0-8077-5240-1 (pbk. : alk. paper)
      1. Academic achievement. I. Title. II. Title: Three dimensions of improving
   student performance.
   LB1062.6.R84   2011
371.26′2—dc22   2011013071

ISBN 978-0-8077-5240-1 (paper)

Printed on acid-free paper

Manufactured in the United States of America

18   17   16   15   14   13   12   11   8   7   6   5   4   3   2   1

It has been said that while some authors like *to write*, many more prefer *to have written*. . . . Writing is a rewarding yet sometimes difficult task. It is also an activity in which real and imagined shortcomings invade awareness at the most inopportune times and disrupt the process. During those times, it is nice to be surrounded by others who can provide support and scaffolding to help ameliorate those lapses. In this case, I am thankful to Jean Ward, who forced me to sit down and put the ideas in this book on paper in spite of my constant excuses. I am thankful to the editorial staff who caught my many errors and inconsistencies. I am especially grateful to my colleagues on the faculty at USC in Educational Psychology area and other areas who provided the intellectual grounding and collaboration that helped develop these ideas, and to the many teachers and students who helped provide a reality check on the ideas presented here. I especially want to thank my parents who sacrificed a great deal to get me through school so many years ago. Lastly, I dedicate this book to my immediate family (Mary, Mariano, Marina, and Vanessa), who had to deal with those long stretches of time when my mind and attention were diverted.

Contents

Foreword

Robert Rueda has accomplished in this book what most educational scholars aspire to but seldom achieve: He has made educational theory practical! And in so doing he has served both his university colleagues and K–12 educators remarkably well. Higher education colleagues will benefit from both the "existence proof" that theory and research can be marshaled to address problems that plague our colleagues in K–12 education (not to mention the equally impressive existence of proof that change is possible within a graduate school of education). K–12 colleagues will benefit from a research-based model of educational reform that is itself driven by an impressive array of research-based principles about learning, pedagogy, culture, and school organization.

As would be the case with any honest model of educational change, Rueda's embraces the complexities of schooling in a very complicated multicultural, multilingual society. Even so, his model of school reform is manageable because it comes packaged in a doubly triadic but accessible (it's not simple but it is transparent and memorable) framework that allows all players in the educational improvement process to keep their wits about them. First is the triad of elements we use to define the primary *goal* of all of our efforts: student learning and performance inside the classroom; it is comprised of *expertise* (both knowledge and skill), *self-regulation* (the capacity to monitor and adjust one's learning tools), and *engagement* (a combination of interest, self-efficacy, and stamina to stay the course in learning tasks). Second is the triad of resources we use as the *means* by which we achieve the learning goal, and not surprisingly, they are, at heart, professional knowledge resources: We are more effective at promoting our goal of student learning to the degree that we possess deep professional knowledge about learning processes, motivation, and organizational/institutional factors that influence our ability to improve teaching and learning. While it sits in the background, the most crucial factor in Rueda's model is context: Both the goals (the learning triad) and the means (the resource triad) are situated within a set of social and cultural practices that permeate all of our activity as learners and teachers. To pretend that those contextual practices don't matter is to guarantee our failure as educational reformers.

Each of these key elements in the two triads are systematically un-packed (chapter 2 for the goal, and chapters 3–5 for each element of professional knowledge) so that we come away with a nuanced understanding of the role each factor plays. In research-based accounts of practice nuance is often another name for complexity and obfuscation, but Rueda manages to avoid both by filtering the nuanced, research-based information provided through the frame of the double triad. As a result, the reader has a chance to develop deep, well organized knowledge of reform tools and processes rather than an ill-structured set of hunches or guesses.

With the knowledge components in place, the ideas all come together in chapter 6, with Rueda sharing vivid glimpses of how the fundamental approach to reform, a version of gap analysis borrowed from reform within the business community, and chapter 7, where he reminds us of what can happen to us when we are insensitive to the social and cultural practices that operate in particular community contexts. What is so impressive in chapter 6 is that we meet all of the basic ideas (the double triad) encountered early on in the book, but now instantiated in examples of real reform efforts, both in higher education and K–12 settings. Here is where we see the real value in an approach grounded in theory and research because we can easily imagine how these ideas might play out in our own institutions. In chapter 7, we learn a basic lesson about context: What we do as human actors trying to improve our collective lot is both cause and consequence of context. We shape and are shaped by the social and cultural practices that operate in the institutional and community contexts within which we work. In providing compelling examples of both success and failure, Rueda reminds me of Tip O'Neal's famous quote about politics—"All politics is local." In chapter 7, we learn that, policy makers' protestations to the contrary, all school reform is local. The failure to make school reform local means that it will be met with resistance or deflected by mock compliance. So reformer beware!

If we put together the themes in Robert Rueda's insightful and useful handbook on school improvement, we arrive at an interesting paradox: We should use a research-based, highly theoretical framework to shape our efforts, but we should implement them as if all that mattered was adapting it to the local context. Metaphorically, it's a variation of the motto of the environmental movement: "Think globally, act locally." And that paradox is, I think, exactly what Rueda wants us to take away from our encounter with his book. I would close by reminding readers that some paradoxes are meant to be embraced. This is one.

—P. David Pearson,
Graduate School of Education, University of California, Berkeley

CHAPTER 1

Introduction and Overview

There are two interesting observations about schools over the last several decades. One is that the students who inhabit American classrooms are rapidly changing, resulting in much more heterogeneous classrooms. The second is that, by almost any objective indicator, there are long-standing and systematic differences in outcomes, especially related to ethnicity, race, language, and socioeconomic status. These characteristics form the backdrop for the current educational landscape, and are likewise important areas of focus in the remainder of this book. A brief look at these patterns is presented below.

THE CHANGING FACE OF AMERICAN CLASSROOMS

There have been significant changes in the students who attend American schools. For example, the percentage of racially/ethnically diverse students enrolled in the nation's public schools increased from 22% in 1972 to 31% in 1986, and to 43% in 2006. This increase in diverse enrollment largely reflects the growth in the percentage of students who were Latino(a).[1] In 2006, Hispanic students represented 20% of public school enrollment, up from 6% in 1972 and 11% in 1986. Between 1979 and 2006, the number of school-age children (ages 5–17) who spoke a language other than English at home increased from 3.8 to 10.8 million, or from 9% to 20% of the population in this age range. Among these children, the percentage who spoke English with difficulty increased from 3% to 6% between 1979 and 2000 (Planty et al., 2008).

The increase in the number of English Learners is especially notable. According to the 2000 census, nearly one in five Americans

> Long-standing and systematic differences in outcomes, especially related to ethnicity, race, language, and socioeconomic status, form the backdrop for the current educational landscape.

speaks a language other than English at home, an increase of nearly 50% from the previous decade (U.S. Department of Education, 2003). This increase, not surprisingly, has been mirrored in the classroom. In 1992, 15% of U.S. teachers were estimated to have at least one English Learner (EL) in their respective classrooms. Ten years later, in 2002, the percentage of U.S. teachers who had at least one EL student in their classroom was 43% (U.S. Department of Education, 2003). Most EL students in the United States (79%) speak Spanish as their primary language (Gandara, Rumberger, Maxwell-Jolly, & Callahan, 2003). In 2003–2004, EL services were provided to 3.8 million students (11% of all students). California and Texas had the largest reported number of students receiving EL services. In California, there were 1.6 million students (26% of all students) who received EL services, while in Texas the number was 0.7 million (16% of all students) (U.S. Department of Education, 2006).

Diversity in American classrooms should not be taken as a negative development. In fact, in many ways, it can be seen as resource (Gonzalez, Moll, & Amanti, 2005). However, despite the fact that diversity by itself is not a reason for concern, the fact that it is related to systematic differences in education outcomes should definitely be a source of concern. A look at some of these patterns related to achievement is presented below.

VARIATION IN EDUCATIONAL OUTCOMES

While large-scale standardized tests are often criticized regarding their immediate usefulness in informing instructional practices, as well as for other reasons (Moss, Girard, & Haniford, 2006), they do offer one source of information regarding educational outcomes, especially from a longitudinal perspective. The National Assessment of Educational Progress (NAEP), for example, has assessed student reading and mathematics performance since the early 1990s. NAEP thus provides a picture of the extent to which student performance in each subject has changed over time, including the achievement gaps between White and Black and between White and Hispanic students.

NAEP data indicate that long-standing differences continue to characterize educational outcomes. For example, in the area of reading, the gap between White and Hispanic 4th-graders did not change measurably in 2007 compared with 1992. Comparing 2007 educational outcomes for White, Hispanic, and Black students at the 4th-grade level, Blacks scored, on average, 27 points lower than Whites (on a 0–500 point scale), and

Hispanics scored, on average, 26 points lower than Whites. At 8th grade, there was no measurable change in the White-Black or White-Hispanic reading achievement gaps in 2007 when compared with 1992 or 2005. In 2007, at the 8th-grade level, Blacks scored, on average, 27 points lower on the reading assessment than Whites, and Hispanics scored, on average, 25 points lower than Whites (Planty et al., 2008). A graphic representation of these patterns is provided in Figure 1.1.

Figure 1.1. Achievement gap differences in White-Black and White-Hispanic 4th- and 8th-grade average reading and mathematics scale scores: 1990–2007

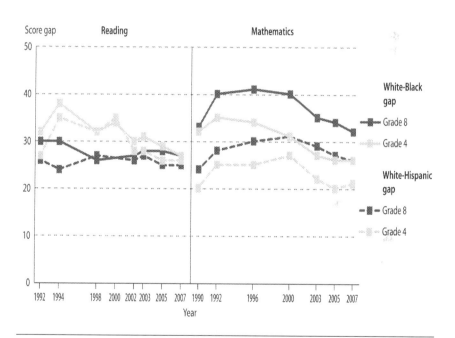

Note: NAEP scores are calculated on a 0 to 500 point scale. Student assessments are not designed to permit comparisons across subjects or grades. Race categories exclude persons of Hispanic ethnicity. The score gap is determined by subtracting the average Black and Hispanic score, respectively, from the average White score. Testing accommodations (e.g., extended time, small-group testing) for children with disabilities and limited-English-proficient students were not permitted from 1990 through 1994. Beginning in 2002, the NAEP national sample for grades 4 and 8 was obtained by aggregating samples from each state, rather than by obtaining an independently selected national sample. See supplemental note 4 for more information on NAEP. *Source*: Planty et al., 2008, p. 26

Similarly, in the area of mathematics, the achievement gap between White and Black 4th-graders was lower in 2007 than in 1990 (26 vs. 32 points), but there was no measurable change over the last 2 years. The gap between White and Hispanic 4th-graders increased in the 1990s before decreasing in the first half of the 2000s, but the gap in 2007 (21 points) was not measurably different from that in 1990. Among 8th-graders, a similar trend existed in both the White-Black and White-Hispanic score gaps: Increases occurred in the 1990s before decreasing to the current levels, which are not measurably different from those in 1990. The White-Black 8th-grade mathematics gap was lower in 2007 than in 2005, but there was no measurable change in the White-Hispanic gap. In 2007, among 8th-graders, the White-Black mathematics gap was 32 points, and the White-Hispanic gap was 26 points (Planty et al., 2008).

In addition, the results of NAEP data from 2005 indicate that nearly half (46%) of 4th-grade students in the EL category scored "below basic" in mathematics—the lowest possible level; with nearly three-quarters (73%) scoring below basic in reading. Middle school achievement in mathematics and reading were also very low, with more than two-thirds (71%) of 8th-grade ELs scoring below basic in math and an equal percentage of these students scoring below basic in reading (Fry, 2007).

These patterns are also associated with poverty. For example, in 2005, the average NAEP score on the 4th-grade mathematics assessment decreased as the percentage of students in the school who were eligible for the school lunch program increased. Students in the highest poverty public schools (those with more than 75% of students eligible for the school lunch program) had an average score of 221, compared with an average score of 255 for students in public schools with the lowest percentage of students in poverty (those with 10% or less of students eligible) (Lutkus, Grigg, & Donohue, 2007). In addition, poverty is related to factors such as race, ethnicity, and access to resources, which translate into opportunity to learn. Comparing schools with different concentrations of poverty reveals that the highest-poverty public schools in 2005 differed from other public schools in terms of particular student characteristics. For example, they had the lowest percentage of White students, the highest percentage of Black and Hispanic students, and the highest percentage of students who reported always speaking a language other than English at home. They also had the highest percentage of 4th-graders who were taught by a teacher with less than 5 years of teaching experience (Lutkus, Grigg, & Donohue, 2007).

EFFORTS TO ADDRESS LOW ACHIEVEMENT

Understandably, educators and the public in general are greatly concerned by these data. There have been a number of approaches that have been developed and implemented in order to change educational outcomes. A brief and nonexhaustive list includes:

- *Increased accountability*—This is best exemplified by the federal education law, No Child Left Behind, which holds states, districts, and schools accountable for student achievement based on standardized test scores (Linn, 2000, 2003), although individual states have implemented their own parallel systems.
- *Professionalization of teachers*—A strong argument has been made that one way to close the achievement gap is to bolster and professionalize the teaching force. It has been argued that there is a close association between teacher quality and student outcomes, and that the most needy students are those who often have the least access to the most qualified teachers (Agarao-Fernandez & de Guzman, 2006; Carnegie Task Force on Teaching as a Profession, 1986; Darling-Hammond & Sykes, 2003).
- *Instructional innovations and research-based interventions*—This is exemplified by the magnitude of approaches to improving instruction that have been developed over the past few decades, especially in the areas of reading, mathematics, and science (see, for example, Dobb, 2004; Lee, 2005). In addition, a major focus of recent federal education policy has been on encouraging approaches that are research-based, with the assumption that many school practices are based on untested or ineffective approaches. Federal funding—Reading First legislation, for example—exemplified this approach to reducing achievement gaps, as do specific instructional interventions, such as Response to Intervention (RTI) and other approaches aimed specifically at language learning issues (Echevarria, Vogt, & Short, 2008) or designed to address cultural issues and low school achievement (Lee, 2005, 2007).
- *Standardization of curriculum and/or teaching practice*—This approach is based on the notion that lack of consistency and coordination of curriculum leads to lower achievement. One approach has been to mandate the nature of either curriculum or teaching approaches (Horn, 2007). For example, in some school districts

such as Los Angeles, low-achieving schools were mandated to use a particular commercial reading program, with an emphasis on fidelity of implementation.

- *Financial incentives*—Financial incentives, for example in the form of teacher bonuses or pay-for-performance programs for students have been seen as a useful strategy in some settings (Lankford, Loeb, & Wyckoff, 2002; Steele, Murnane, & Willet, 2009).

- *Privatization*—One approach to narrowing the achievement gap, often with a business-oriented perspective on education, is to provide alternatives to public schools, most clearly seen in the growth of charter schools (U.S. Department of Education, Office of Innovation and Improvement, 2006), initiatives such as Race to the Top (RTT) funding of innovative programs and schools, and the growth of private educational systems through vouchers or other systems (Boyles, 2005; Levin, 2001).

- *Legislation*—Partly fueled by public mistrust of the education bureaucracy, there is some support for deciding important educational policy issues through popular vote. In some cases, this has resulted in the decisionmaking authority being removed from the educational establishment altogether. For example, in California, the controversy over bilingual instruction in public schools was developed into a ballot initiative, which let voters decide which language instructional approach would be allowed in public schools. Proposition 227 in California, passed by voters in 1998, as well as related initiatives in Arizona and Massachusetts, are examples of this approach (Gandara & Gomez, 2009), as are legislative efforts aimed at reduced class size (Stecher, McCaffrey, & Bugliari, 2003).

- *School restructuring/reform*—There are a wide range of both local and national efforts that try to bring about change through modifying structural or organizational features of schools, including:
    Changing the governance structure of the school either to diminish school-based management and decisionmaking or to increase control, monitoring, and oversight by the Local Education Agency (LEA);
    Closing the school and reopening it as a focus or theme school, with new staff or staff skilled in the focus area;
    Reconstituting the school into smaller autonomous learning communities;

Dissolving the school and assigning students to other
schools in the district;

Pairing the school in restructuring with a higher-perform-
ing school; or

Expanding or narrowing the grades served (Hassel, Hassel,
& Rhim, 2007).

The range of approaches is also exemplified on the organizational side by initiatives such as reduced class size or the reorganization of governance, and on the curricular side by CSR (Comprehensive School Reform) programs such as Success For All (SFA), Accelerated Schools (AS), Core Knowledge (CK), and Direct Instruction (DI) (Datnow, Hubbard, & Mehan, 2002; Datnow, Lasky, Stringfield, & Tedlie, 2005; Gandara, 2005; Vernez, Karam, Mariano, & DeMartini, 2006).

> In spite of noteworthy attempts to remedy disparities in student performance, success is modest except in isolated settings or on narrowly derived outcomes. The three primary reasons for this include 1. the fragmentation of approaches, 2. the misalignment of approaches and goals, and 3. the failure to match solutions to problems.

In spite of these and other noteworthy attempts to remedy disparities in student performance, success is modest except in isolated settings or on narrowly derived outcomes. The central thesis in this book is that there are three primary reasons. These include 1. the fragmentation of approaches, 2. the misalignment of approaches and goals, and 3. the failure to match solutions to problems.

The Problem of Fragmentation

The fragmentation is in part due to how the knowledge and theories underlying this work are organized—by discipline and by theories within disciplines. These disciplinary lines are often carried over into places like universities and into the journals and publications that are used to disseminate new knowledge. It is very hard to break these virtual chains that serve to filter how problems and solutions are conceived and addressed. Learning theorists tend to focus on internal cognitive processes and the architectural features of the cognitive system; motivation theorists tend to focus on the beliefs and affective factors individuals have about things

Figure 1.2. The 3 dimensions that impact the goal of engaged, expert, self-
    regulating learners

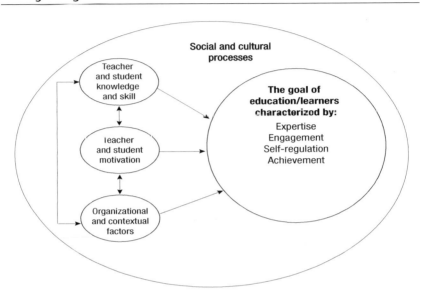

Note: At the core of the figure is the ideal result of schooling—a learner who has developed expertise in a variety of areas, who can self-regulate his or her own learning and motivation and adjust accordingly, and who is able to perform to the best of his or her ability.

like specific tasks and their ability to succeed; sociocultural theorists tend to focus on features of context and cultural processes; and organizational theorists focus on the structures and processes of organizations and institutions and how they can influence performance. While all of these provide valid perspectives on behavior and functioning, given the complexity of many current educational and social issues, none comprehensively address all of the relevant dimensions. These dimensions, represented in Figure 1.2, will be described more fully in Chapter 2 and elsewhere in the book. However, a major argument is that none take precedence—they must all be considered in order to maximize performance and reduce inequitable outcomes.

> Sometimes a problem is seen as having been addressed when a solution has been implemented—regardless of the correspondence between the solution and the actual problem, or of the eventual outcome of the solution.

The Problems of Misalignment and Mismatch

The misalignment problem relates to the fact that there are several levels of goals or approaches within any particular work or educational setting. Unless careful consideration is given, changes at one level may have unforeseen consequences for those at another level, or may even work at cross-purposes. A good example is found in the move by some districts to assure quality instruction by mandating standardization of approaches in low-achieving schools and classrooms. While certain cognitive and instructional goals may be met in this fashion, the motivational consequences of diminished autonomy for highly skilled teachers are sometimes an unintended consequence (e.g., Stevenson, 2008).

> It sounds contrary to common sense, but often when a problem such as low achievement exists, solutions (programs, projects, new approaches) are instituted without really understanding why the problem existed in the first place.

Failing to Match Solutions with Problems

A not unrelated problem is the mismatch between problems and solutions, in part due to a tendency to take action based on assumed causes. Sometimes a problem is seen as having been addressed when a solution has been implemented—regardless of the correspondence between the solution and the actual problem, or of the eventual outcome of the solution. This is sometimes due to organizational or institutional practices that reward action rather than results. Solutions to addressing inequitable outcomes must be matched to the problem in a specific social context. Many schools are inundated by programs and projects to such a degree that they have been referred to as *laminated*—such as when a worker in a remodeling project strips off one layer of a countertop only to find layers and layers underneath. It sounds contrary to common sense, but often when

> Many times a problem is considered to be addressed once a solution is in place—irrespective of how well it works.

a problem such as low achievement exists, solutions (programs, projects, new approaches) are instituted without really understanding why the problem existed in the first place. Part of this is due to the fact that comprehensive frameworks that permit a wider lens on the problem are not typically considered. More importantly, many times the organizational dynamics are such that a problem is considered to be addressed once a solution is in place—irrespective of how well it works. Therefore a systematic process of examining possible causes of performance issues using a comprehensive framework is called for.

> The problems that characterize urban schools are sufficiently complex that a more comprehensive approach is needed.

Table 1.1. Factors impacting student outcomes in reading

Between Reader	Within Reader	Sociocultural	Group
• Word recognition • Fluency • General vocabulary • Oral language ability • Linguistic knowledge • Discourse knowledge • Background knowledge • Strategies • Cognitive abilities (e.g., attention, working memory, etc.) • Metacognitive ability • Motivation • Attitude toward reading • Identity as reader	• Domain-specific vocabulary • Domain-specific knowledge • Text/context-specific motivation • Text/context-specific attitude • Text/context-specific purposes • Text/context-specific activity • Text (e.g., topic, difficulty, etc.) • Medium (e.g., multimedia, book, article, chart, poem, etc.) • Assessment used (formal, informal, group, individual, answer-choice format) • Context	• Cultural membership • Discourse community • Ideology • Social practices	• Linguistic group • Ethnicity • Race • Socioeconomic status • Public or private school • School quality

Source: Snow, C. E. & Biancarosa, G., 2003

WHAT IS THE RIGHT FRAMEWORK TO ADDRESS THE ISSUES?

With regard to the frameworks that are often used to address differences in school performance among different groups of students, too often the question is asked, "Which of these is the right perspective?" The answer to this question frames the two main points of this book. The first point is that there is no "right" perspective. The problems that characterize urban schools are sufficiently complex that a more comprehensive approach is needed than is often used now. As an example, it is instructive to look at the factors that the National Reading Panel specified as having an impact on the single domain of reading comprehension (see Table 1.1). It is clear that this set of factors spans a wide range that is unlikely to be addressed by any single perspective.

Each of these frameworks to be described in the following chapter offers valuable insights into performance, but none by itself is sufficient to address the complexities and range of problems that serve to create the systematic and long-standing differences in achievement that were described earlier. Thus a comprehensive or multidimensional approach is needed. A central point is that the framework and information to be presented is derived from established work in education, psychology, anthropology, and organizational theory. However, what is different is that the perspective to be advocated here promotes a comprehensive framework drawing from all of these fields, in a way that is not normally done, for the purpose of examining student and school outcomes, and tries to assist in the task of applying the best of what is already known in useful ways to improve those outcomes.

> The successful learner who displays three key features represents the endpoint and the goal of education. This learner: 1. is able to perform in a self-regulated fashion, 2. is engaged, and 3. has developed expertise.

THE ULTIMATE GOAL OF SCHOOLING

Figure 1.2 provides a multidimensional model, which forms the foundation of this book. The successful learner who displays three key features represents the endpoint and the goal of education. This learner: 1. is able to perform in a self-regulated fashion, 2. is engaged, and 3. has developed expertise. This is a learner who has developed expertise in a variety

> There are three primary influences on the improvement of student development and performance: 1. learning processes and factors, 2. motivational factors, and 3. organizational and institutional factors. Social and cultural processes permeate all of the other aspects of the model.

of areas, who can self-regulate his or her own learning and motivation and adjust accordingly, and who is able to perform to the best of his or her ability.

The factors that research has shown to be critical in this endeavor are grouped in to three areas, although they are highly interrelated. These include learning characteristics of individual students, such as prior knowledge, use of learning strategies, metacognitive skills, and so forth. While these are given the most attention in most school settings, motivational factors are equally important and highly related to learning. These include factors such as self-efficacy, interest, value, goal orientation, attributions, and other motivational factors, all of which are highly related to the cultural settings to which one has been exposed. Finally, there are what are loosely termed organizational/institutional/community factors. This is the broadest area, and includes factors related to organizations such as schools, including administrative policies and practices, organizational culture, as well as factors outside of these settings like community or wider socio-political factors. Thus, there are three primary influences on the improvement of student development and performance: 1. learning processes and factors, 2. motivational factors, and 3. organizational and institutional factors. Social and cultural processes permeate all of the other aspects of the model.

Since teaching and learning are the fundamental priorities of schools and educational institutions, a comprehensive discussion of learning processes will be provided, and the interaction of each of these elements will be elaborated in the book.

The impetus for this volume is based on work with educational practitioners in my role as a professor at a major research university (the University of Southern California). While the university traditionally had a reputation for having a strong program for school leaders, the relevance and effectiveness of the program began to be questioned. Questions were raised about the ability of the program to prepare school leaders equipped to deal with the more complex and demanding challenges currently facing urban schools. Thus, when the School of Education undertook an analysis and reorganization of its doctoral programs, it also took that opportunity to strengthen and focus its program toward the ultimate goal of improvement in schools and educational organizations. A more complete description of the change process that took place is provided in Chapter 5. However, an important element of the new approach in the coursework was to adopt a problem-solving model developed by one of our own faculty (Clark & Estes, 2008), called *gap analysis,* as a means to combine theory and practice.

While the gap analysis approach was originally focused on business and organizational settings, we have found it applicable to a wide range of contexts, including the school contexts, which are the focus of this volume. This book, then, represents many of the lessons learned over the years that have passed since the new program was developed, including my work on the learning team, working with doctoral students to implement and build on the ideas presented in the following chapters in their own K–12 schools and other educational settings, and guiding dissertation work.

In sum, the book proposes a multidimensional model that helps provide a more comprehensive lens for considering achievement differences in schools and other educational settings. It provides a brief overview of the key theories and findings in the specific domains the model encompasses. In addition, the book suggests a problem-solving framework that helps align solutions to the causes of problems, thus avoiding the common mistakes of focusing too narrowly on the issues or of generating solutions without understanding the causes. The goal is to help practitioners bridge these often disparate areas and provide a wider, more comprehensive, and more coordinated lens for considering and ultimately reducing achievement differences.

CHAPTER 2

A Focus on Learning and Related Outcomes: Where Do We Want to End Up?

While it may appear to be somewhat out of order, this chapter begins with a focus on the endpoint, as described in Figure 1.2 and text in the last chapter: the engaged, self-regulating learner. Since an important part of the model has to do with the goals that one starts out with in attempts to improve school outcomes, it is important to know what those goals are. In this chapter, we focus on academic outcomes. But what does that really mean? It is worth taking a few moments to try to specify in more detail what meaningful, desirable, and realistic outcomes are for students.

ACHIEVEMENT

What is it that we would like students to be able to do and know when they leave school? What kinds of learners should schools produce? These questions have long occupied a variety of different groups concerned with schools and the educational system. The answers to these questions have been wide in scope, and have ranged from promoting particular values and perspectives, to preparing students for roles related to civic participation and success in a global society, to mastery of specific facts, to mastery of specific content standards. Regardless of the diversity of opinion on this issue, most would agree on the goals of assuring that students achieve basic academic goals and that schools produce literate graduates. The most recent national standards are an attempt to formalize those goals, as represented by the Common Core State Standards Initiative, headed by the National Governors Association and the Council of Chief State School Officers (see http://www.corestandards.org/). The standards apply to

> Achievement can be conceived of as the mastery of domain specific content knowledge as reflected in a variety of measures and in different contexts.

English language arts, history, social studies, science, and math, and include specific goals, separated by grade and subject.

Another approach to specifying educational goals is based on an accountability approach. That is, what students should know is represented by what is reflected on formal assessments and how students compare to others in a specified reference group. This approach has been a highly salient feature of the educational landscape in recent years, and has been used as a major tool in educational reform. There is much discussion, and not an insignificant amount of controversy, about accountability, however; and as the debate seems to suggest, "The devil is in the details." At the narrowest end of the continuum, success is defined as scores on a standardized assessment. That is a very narrow definition, however, and one that has been much criticized (Cochran-Smith & Lytle, 2006) for limiting both what students should aspire to as well as what schools should focus on in assisting them. If that is *not* the only or most important factor, what is? In addition, given the sizable inequitable outcomes noted in the previous chapter, how should we think of reasonable goals for schooling? One approach, the one adopted here, is that achievement can be conceived of as the mastery of domain specific content knowledge as reflected in a variety of measures and in different contexts. When achievement is assessed through a variety of indicators, it helps minimize the tendency to view it in terms of narrow content on a single measure. When it is required to apply to a variety of domains and contexts, it minimizes the tendency to foster knowledge and skills that apply nowhere else other than the classroom.

This chapter looks in greater depth at the three features identified in Chapter 1 that characterize the ideal learners that we hope to develop and foster in our schools, characteristics that are proposed for consideration as wide-ranging educational goals. They include self-regulation, expertise, and engagement. Each of these will be briefly described in the following section.

SELF-REGULATION

It is clear that schools and the education system in general are a common target of public dissatisfaction. As noted earlier, there have been many different approaches to address the real and perceived issues believed to be problematic. A look at the range of many of the approaches that have been tried, however, shows that they seem to be focused on changing the goals, structure, or processes of schooling in ways that focus on doing something *to students*. That is, students often seem to be considered as passive recipients of the many efforts to achieve better results in schools. Yet there is a competing view— one that builds on a good deal of work in educational psychology and other areas indicating that a primary goal of

> A major goal of a good education is to produce self-regulated learners who have acquired expertise and can transfer their knowledge and skills to real world problems. Students who are self-regulating can compensate for and overcome many problems even under imperfect learning conditions, and very similar to the kinds of students or individuals that are sometimes referred to as resilient.

schooling should be to enhance students' self-regulatory skills. That is, a major goal of a good education is to produce self-regulated learners who have acquired expertise and can transfer their knowledge and skills to real world problems (Rueda & Dembo, 2006). Students who are self-regulating can compensate for and overcome many problems, even under imperfect learning conditions and in less than adequate learning contexts. Notice that this sounds very similar to the kinds of students or individuals who are sometimes referred to as *resilient*. They are able to do and achieve things when others in similar circumstances are not, even under less than ideal conditions.

There is a significant amount of research that suggests the importance of self-regulatory skills in academic achievement (Zimmerman, 1990, 2008; Zimmerman & Schunk, 2001). Self-regulation is defined as "self-generated thoughts, feelings, and actions that are planned and cyclically adapted to the attainment of personal goals" (Zimmerman, 2000, p. 14). Research also indicates that students who self-monitor their learning progress and engagement with tasks, generate internal feedback (Zimmerman & Cleary, 2009). This internal feedback works to help assess possible gaps in one's performance, and the result may improve learning outcomes (Azevedo & Cromley, 2004; Butler & Winne, 1995; Ley &Young, 2001). In addition, students who are capable of effective learning tend to choose appropriate learning goals and to use adaptive knowledge and skills to direct their learning. These students are also able to select effective learning strategies appropriate to the task at hand. In other words, they are able to regulate

> Students who are capable of effective learning are able to regulate their learning and take responsibility for the acquisition and maintenance of new skills.

their learning and take responsibility for the acquisition and maintenance of new skills.

One of the central aspects of self-regulated learning is students' ability to select, combine, and coordinate learning activities (Zimmerman & Martinez-Pons, 1990). The cognitive aspects of effective self-regulated learning are elaboration (e.g., exploring how the information might be useful in the real world) and control strategies. In addition, effective learning requires adaptive motivational beliefs related to factors such as self-efficacy, interest, goal orientation, attributions, and other variables, which in turn affect effort and persistence in learning. There is a significant body of research findings that support the connection among motivational variables, learning strategies, self-regulatory behavior, and academic achievement (Bandura, 1997; Deci & Ryan, 1985; Zimmerman, 2000). For this reason, it is likely that students who have acquired self-regulatory ability are able to reduce the impact of less than optimal school and learning environments.

EXPERTISE

There is a long history in the educational literature of reliance on a deficit model, especially when it comes to students who are different based on socioeconomic status, ethnicity, language, culture, and other factors that often characterize students in urban school settings. This has often been exemplified and instantiated through the use of ability and intelligence assessments (Valencia, 2010). Ability, assumed to be the primary mediator of school and academic success, has often been seen as fixed and, in the most egregious cases, as linked to factors such as socioeconomic status, ethnicity, and race (Herrnstein & Murray, 1994). However, recent work in the area of expertise may hold much more importance to school outcomes, and especially with the ability of schools to influence it (Feldon, 2007; Hatano & Oura, 2003). While there is not complete agreement about the exact nature of expertise, or whether it is the same across all domains (Feldon, 2008), it appears to be a useful concept when thinking about educational goals.

> Students who have acquired self-regulatory ability are able to reduce the impact of less than optimal school and learning environments.

The work in expertise has been an outgrowth of the interest in cognitive psychology regarding the question, "What is it that differentiates experts from novices?" In the past it had been assumed that an expert's performance in a given activity or task was due to increased knowledge gained by training and accumulated experience. However, it became clear that sometimes experts' decisions were no more accurate than those of beginners' (Bolger & Wright,

> Evidence suggests that in those domains where performance consistently increases, aspiring experts seek out and engage in particular kinds of experience, that is, deliberate practice— activities designed for the sole purpose of effectively improving specific aspects of an individual's performance.

1992). Performance in a given domain or on a specific activity often increases as a function of experience—up to a point. Beyond this point, however, further improvements are much less frequent and stable, and the amount of experience becomes a poor predictor of attained performance (Ericsson & Lehmann, 1996). Simply putting in time does not make one an expert, and continued improvement is not an automatic consequences of more experience. I am sure we are all aware of the difference between the "experienced" teacher who has the same year of experience repeated over 20 years, and the "experienced" teacher who exerted significant effort over 20 years to be a highly effective teacher. Rather, the evidence suggests that in those domains where performance consistently increases, aspiring experts seek out and engage in particular kinds of experience, that is, deliberate practice (Ericsson, Krampe & Tesch-Römer, 1993)—activities designed for the sole purpose of effectively improving specific aspects of an individual's performance. For example, the critical difference among expert musicians differing in the level of attained solo performance concerned the amounts of time they had spent in solitary practice during their music development, which totaled around 10,000 hours by age 20 for the best experts, around 5,000 hours for the least accomplished expert musicians, and only 2,000 hours for serious amateur pianists. Generally, the accumulated amount of deliberate practice, *deliberate* being a key descriptor, is closely related to the attained level of performance of many types of experts, such as musicians (Ericsson et al., 1993; Sloboda, Davidson, Howe, & Moore, 1996), chess players (Charness, Krampe & Mayr, 1996), and athletes (Starkes, Deakin, Allard, Hodges, & Hayes, 1996).

What this work has shown is that the difference between experts and nonexperts is not just the amount and complexity of the knowledge

> The difference between experts and nonexperts is not just the amount and complexity of the knowledge they have accumulated, but rather qualitative differences in the organization of knowledqe and how it is represented.

they have accumulated, but rather qualitative differences in the organization of knowledge and how it is represented (Chi, Glaser, & Rees, 1982). They are able to rapidly and reliably retrieve relevant information whenever it is applicable. For these reasons, they can adapt rapidly to changing circumstances and anticipate future events, which in turn help them to constantly monitor and evaluate their own performance (Ericsson, 1998; Glaser, 1996) so they can keep improving their own performance by designing their own training and assimilating new knowledge.

In a report by the National Research Council, Bransford, Brown, and Cocking (1999) summarized the key aspects of expertise that suggest the effects of successful learning:

- Experts notice features and meaningful patterns of information that are not noticed by novices
- Experts have acquired a great deal of content knowledge that is organized, and their organization of information reflects a deep understanding of the subject matter
- Experts' knowledge cannot be reduced to sets of isolated facts or propositions but, instead reflects contexts of applicability, i.e., it is *conditionalized*
- Experts are able to retrieve important aspects of their knowledge with little effort
- Though experts know their disciplines thoroughly, this does not guarantee that they are able to instruct others about the topic
- Experts have varying levels of flexibility in their approaches to new situations. (p. xiii)

Consistent with these features, some researchers in the area of expertise have differentiated *adaptive* experts from *routine* experts (Hatano & Inagaki, 2000). Adaptive experts are those who not only understand why their particular skills are effective, but who also can adapt their skills to new demands as tasks change, or invent new procedures as needed. For our purposes, it is important to recognize that while ability may play a role in eventual school and life outcomes, other factors such as deliberate practice and sustained effort are much more impor- | Studies of expertise consistently find that there is no correlation between IQ and experts' performance (Ericsson, 1998; Ericsson & Charness, 1994; Ericsson & Lehmann, 1996). Expertise can be created, and while an individual needs to select in what domains he or she will become an expert, it is important to know that experts are created, not born.

> Studies of expertise consistently find that there is no correlation between IQ and experts' performance.

ENGAGEMENT

As the following chapters will argue, motivation is a key aspect of performance in school as well as in other domains. One indication that a person is motivated is the degree to which they get involved and immersed in an activity or task. Recent work that has begun to focus on this area often adopted the term *engagement* (Fredericks, Blumenfeld, & Paris, 2004). However, the concept of engagement is relatively new and researchers are exploring the best ways to define and operationalize this construct (Fredericks, Blumenfeld, & Paris, 2004; Furrer & Skinner, 2003; Jimerson, Campus, & Greif, 2003; Skinner, Furrer, Marchand, & Kindermann, 2008).

In a recent review on this topic, Fredericks and colleagues proposed that engagement is a multidimensional construct including behavioral engagement (actively performing learning activities), cognitive engagement (using cognitive strategies to foster deep learning), and affective engagement (expressing enjoyment about learning). Other researchers such as Furrer and Skinner (2003), and Skinner and colleagues (2008) included both behavioral (e.g., working hard and trying) and affective dimensions (e.g., enjoyment of learning, involvement, and interest) in their definition of engagement as "active, goal-directed, flexible, constructive, persistent, focused interactions with the social and physical environments" (Furrer & Skinner, 2008, p. 149). Other researchers have focused less on the affective aspects of engagement in favor of behavioral and cognitive aspects such as concentration, effort, use of cognitive strategies and metacognitive strategies such as planning and monitoring, and persistence during the initiation and execution of a cognitive task (Cox & Guthrie, 2001; Furrer & Skinner, 2003; Guthrie &

> One indication that a person is motivated is the degree to which they get involved and immersed in an activity or task.

> Motivational beliefs and processes largely drive engagement. In general, these receive much less systematic attention in schools and classrooms than the development of skills, although learning and motivation are intricately linked.

Wigfield, 2000; Kirsch, de Jong, LaFontaine, McQueen, Mendelovits, & Monseur, 2002; Meece, Blumenfeld, & Hoyle, 1988, Skinner, Zimmer-Gembeck, & Connell , 1998).

As we will see later, motivational beliefs and processes largely drive engagement. In general, these receive much less systematic attention in schools and classrooms than the development of skills, although learning and motivation are intricately linked in a variety of ways. In any case, it can be argued that engagement is both an outcome in itself as well as a mediator of other learning and achievement outcomes. However, just the fact that an individual is highly engaged does not automatically lead to positive outcomes. Many students exhibit high degrees of engagement in *not* learning, in being disruptive, resistant to learning, and so forth (Skinner, Furrer, Marchand, & Kindermann, 2008). In one study, for example, we noted that 5th-grade students who were learning English in California public schools spent a great deal of time and effort, and were quite strategic, in *appearing* to be proficient in English (Monzo & Rueda, 2009). These students were reacting in an adaptive fashion to larger social pressures in that context that consider limited English proficiency as a social stigma, and were quite engaged in their efforts to appear competent to the teacher and their English-speaking peers. These students were engaged, but not with tasks that were likely to promote positive academic outcomes. Thus, engagement should not be seen as in a vacuum, rather it is always directed toward the achievement of one or more goals. Choosing the right goals is therefore highly important, and it is important that engagement be directed toward meaningful and rewarding goals. Given that one has embraced meaningful goals, engagement is an important factor in achieving those goals.

While the focus in this volume is on school success, education does not have much value unless it facilitates the achievement of important life goals as well. Thus, there is another nuance of the notion of engagement—toward larger social, community, and civic goals that characterize productive and fulfilled citizens in the larger social world (Kezar, Chambers, & Burkhardt, 2005;

> Engagement should not be seen as in a vacuum, and it is important that engagement be directed toward meaningful and rewarding goals.

Longo, 2007). There is some evidence from national surveys that students who have experienced civic education are more likely than other students to be able to interpret political information critically, to discuss political issues with peers and adults, to monitor the news, and to feel confident about their ability to speak in

> Education does not have much value unless it facilitates the achievement of important life goals.

public (Comber, 2005). Other evidence suggests that students with these types of experiences show better ability to clearly express opinions, better collaborative group skills, and better ability to work in culturally diverse teams (Torney-Purta and Wilkenfeld, 2009).

These are critically important 21st-century skills that students need for future success. In addition, from an equity perspective, these findings are important, because amount of education, income, ethnicity, and immigration status are all strong predictors of civic participation and civic skill acquisition (Kahne & Middaugh, 2008). Access to these types of civic learning opportunities may also be linked to later academic outcomes such as whether students choose to stay in school or drop out (Davila & Mora, 2007).

The following chapters build on these ideas and look at the factors that can reasonably be expected to contribute to the goals discussed here.

> There is some evidence from national surveys that students who have experienced civic education show better ability to clearly express opinions, better collaborative group skills, and better ability to work in culturally diverse teams.

CHAPTER 3

The Learning
and Knowledge Dimension

Consider the following array of educational issues:

- What students learn in school has no connection to real-world problems
- Students are unable to use what they learn in school
- During the summer, students forget what they learned
- Students and parents in many urban schools do not know how to prepare for college
- Teachers are not clear on how to implement new Response to Intervention procedures
- Parents are unsure how to participate in their child's education
- Teachers and administrators are unsure how to deal with huge changes in demographics at their school
- Teachers are unsure how to provide effective instruction for students who do not speak English
- Students go to college without having mastered the skills needed to study effectively
- Some students can decode words but have problems comprehending what they read

What do these (and many other similar) educational problems have in common? They involve issues of learning and knowledge gaps related to what people need in order to function effectively. When these issues involve students, these types of issues in school performance are often lumped under the label of *learning problems*. However, as the list suggests, learning issues are hardly confined to students. But what is learning?

Certainly most people, when asked about education, will include teaching and learning as part of their central idea of what schooling involves. There is no shortage of definitions of what learning is, and different theoretical orientations in the existing literature emphasize different aspects of the processes involved (Alexander, Schallert, & Reynolds, 2009; Meltzoff, Kuhl, Movellan, & Sejnowski, 2009). For example, *behavioral approaches* emphasize learning as changes in behavior as a function of environmental contingencies in voluntary (or operant) behaviors over which we have control, such as sitting in a chair or standing up. It also focuses on the strength of associations between environmental stimuli and behaviors that we do not typically control (respondent), such as nausea at the sight of something unpleasant. *Social cognitive approaches* focus on the triarchic relationships among the constellation of *person-behavior-environment* variables and the ways that each impacts the others. While environmental factors are still important, the critical factor is how the individual perceives and interprets them, thus explaining why the *same* environmental events result in *different* behaviors for different individuals. *Cognitive psychology* tends to focus on the internal mental events, processes, and structures that comprise complex thought, problem-solving, and decisionmaking. *Sociocultural and sociohistorical theories* emphasize the cultural and social aspects of learning, the role of social context in impacting behavior, and the role of tools in learning (broadly conceived as anything that helps mediate thinking and learning, from tangible things like computers, to more abstract culturally inherited tools, such as language and the writing system). More recently, *neuropsychological approaches* have begun to look at the underlying neurological processes and structures that are involved in learning and related areas such as emotion. For readers unfamiliar with the different perspectives, there are several useful sources that provide good overviews on learning applied to classrooms in particular, including Alexander (2006); Bransford, Brown, and Cocking (1999); Gredler (2009); Mayer (2008, 2011); Moreno (2010); Ormrod (2010); and Slavin (2009). A highly readable and useful resource is Mayer (2011).

How do these perspectives compare and differ from one another? Which one is *right*? In the academic world, cognitive psychology and increasingly, neuropsychology, are the dominant perspectives. However, the debate about learning theories, even if confined to the question of "what is learning?" could take volumes, as would a comprehensive review of the details of each of the perspectives described. The complex issues embedded in this question are important in the academic world, where researchers and theoreticians struggle with discovering, testing, and refining basic theoretical knowledge about basic learning processes.

While many academics work on applied problems in schools either entirely or in addition to theoretical problems, practitioners in school settings are charged primarily with solving educational problems in schools, and spend most or all of their time solving day-to-day problems. While a solid grounding in the basics of learning theory is essential for this work, it is argued that a pragmatic approach is one best suited to this purpose, and one that will be adopted here.

Mayer (2011) provides a simple yet workable definition of learning as a point of departure: "Learning is a change in knowledge attributable to experience" (p. 14). As Mayer notes, this definition has three main components: learning involves a change in the learner, what is changed is the learner's knowledge, and the cause of the change is the learner's experience. One of the implications of this definition is that a key goal of learning is knowledge. The other implication is that experiences, intentional or otherwise, are key—including classroom instruction, but also things like the social and cultural contexts that schools create for their students. These are discussed in more detail in Chapter 6, but each of these is briefly considered below.

THE KNOWLEDGE DIMENSION

One way to make concrete issues involving teaching and learning is to ask the question, what does one need to know in order to achieve his or her goals? From the perspective of an educational leader, if you are not clear about what those you supervise should know, how can they themselves be clear? This question forces one to consider the issue of knowledge directly. While this may seem like a deceptively simple matter, it is surprisingly more complex in practice when one tries to be concrete and specify exactly what students, teachers, and others should be able to know and do. Consider, for example, all the things that students need to know (both in and out of the classroom) in order to have a successful school experience; what teachers need to know as they struggle with the design and implementation of accountability programs, standards-based curricula, authentic assessments, school reform initiatives, and so forth; what coaches and specialists need to know in supervising the teaching and learning of others; or what administrators need to know in keeping everything running in an effective, orderly fashion and satisfying multiple constituents. Fortunately, there are some helpful guides. One in particular is Bloom's Taxonomy (Bloom, Englehart, Furst, Hill, &

Consider all the things that students need to know (both in and out of the classroom) in order to have a successful school experience; what teachers need to know as they struggle with the design and implementation of accountability programs, standards-based curricula, authentic assessments, school reform initiatives, and so forth; what coaches and specialists need to know in supervising the teaching and learning of others; or what administrators need to know.

Krathwohl, 1956), as well as recent revisions (Anderson & Krathwohl, 2001).

The original work by Bloom focused on three categories: a cognitive domain (mental skills or knowledge), an affective domain (feelings, emotions, attitudes), and psychomotor (manual or physical skills). Because of the relevance to classroom instruction and the outcomes of schooling are assessed, the cognitive domain is the one that received the most attention over the years. The cognitive domain included knowledge, comprehension, application, analysis, synthesis, and evaluation. These were assumed to be in ordinal order, with knowledge of something being the most basic level, and evaluation being the most complex.

One of the contributions of cognitive approaches to learning has been to highlight the different types of knowledge. Anderson & Krathwohl (2001), for example, specify four types:

- *Factual Knowledge* is what is commonly known as facts. It refers to knowledge that is basic to specific disciplines, contexts, or domains. It includes things like terminology, details or elements that one must know or be familiar with in order to understand and function effectively or solve a problem in a given area.
- *Conceptual Knowledge* is knowledge of categories, classifications, principles, generalizations, theories, models, or structures pertinent to a particular area.
- *Procedural Knowledge* refers to knowing how to do something— from driving a car, to knowing how to study, and so forth. It can also refer to methods of inquiry, very specific or finite skills, algorithms, techniques, and particular methodologies that are required to accomplish specific activities.
- *Metacognitive Knowledge* is the awareness of one's own cognition and particular cognitive processes. It is the type of knowledge that allows one to know when and why to do something. It is also a

key aspect of strategic behavior in solving problems, and allows one to consider contextual and conditional aspects of a given activity or problem.

More recent elaborations of the original taxonomy (Anderson & Krathwohl, 2001) have led to the creation of a matrix which includes the intersection of these four types of knowledge as well as six different levels of cognitive processes in which the knowledge might be applied. The cognitive processes (each of which can be elaborated into even finer categories than provided here) include the following:

- *Remember*—recognizing or recalling relevant knowledge from long-term memory
- *Understand*—constructing meaning from oral and written sources
- *Apply*—carrying out or using a procedure in a specific situation
- *Analyze*—breaking something into parts and determining how they relate to one another as well as to an overall structure, framework, or purpose
- *Evaluate*—making judgments and distinctions based on specified criteria and standards
- *Create*—forming a coherent or functional pattern or whole from distinct elements

Anderson and Krathwohl provide a useful elaboration in terms of examples and descriptions of all of the various types of knowledge described by the intersection of the knowledge and cognitive process dimensions of the matrix. As the knowledge matrix (see Table 3.1) makes clear,

Table 3.1. The Anderson and Krathwohl Taxonomy for Teaching, Learning, and Assessing

The Knowledge Dimensions	COGNITIVE PROCESSES					
	1. Remember	2. Understand	3. Apply	4. Analyze	5. Evaluate	6. Create
Factual						
Conceptual						
Procedural						
Metacognitive						

Source: Adapted from Anderson & Krathwohl, 2001

knowing something can mean many things. Consider, for example, the assessment of a child's comprehension of the story *Goldilocks and the 3 Bears*. Determining the child's understanding of the story could focus on any of the following dimensions:

- *Remember*: Describe where Goldilocks lived.
- *Understand*: Summarize what the Goldilocks story was about.
- *Apply*: Construct a theory as to why Goldilocks went into the house.
- *Analyze*: Differentiate between how Goldilocks reacted and how you would react in each story event.
- *Evaluate*: Assess whether you think this really happened to Goldilocks.
- *Create*: Compose a song, skit, poem, or rap to convey the Goldilocks story in a new form.

There are several important implications of this taxonomy that make it useful for improving schools. For example, consider the following areas:

Equity and Challenge

There is an often-referenced biblical phrase in education circles: "For to all those who have, more will be given, and they will have an abundance; but from those who have nothing, even what they have will be taken away" (Matthew, 25:29, *New Revised Standard Version*). The more colloquial version translates as "the rich get richer, and the poor get poorer." In educational terms, this translates into differences in *opportunity to learn.* There are well known differences in the quality of schooling in the educational system. Students in urban schools with large numbers of students who are poor, English Learners, immigrants, and from diverse racial and ethnic backgrounds are especially likely to find themselves in educational settings that may be of lesser quality in terms of physical infrastructure, quality of teachers, level of curricular challenge, and other resources. In terms of knowledge, which can be seen as the stuff of curriculum, they are likely to get less complex, less challenging, and more rote type of activities. In the framework of the taxonomy, the curriculum and activities are more likely to be in the upper left-hand corner than in the bottom right-hand corner. One advantage of using the taxonomy framework is that it helps to highlight and pinpoint these differences when they might not otherwise be obvious.

Instructional Considerations

Differentiating knowledge into distinct categories is more than an academic exercise. There is good evidence that different instructional approaches are more effective for some types of knowledge than others. Moreover, while all types of knowledge are important in learning, some types are more critical to the kinds of goals school ideally would try to promote, such as being able to acquire meaningful learning, apply knowledge to solve problems, and to transfer that knowledge to other settings and types of problems (see Mayer, 2008, especially section II).

Knowing What to Assess

One of the frequent criticisms of standardized tests is that they can reduce what one has learned to easily answerable items that cover small bits of disconnected information. In fact, past efforts to explore the use of portfolios or to assess complex knowledge are in part due to the dissatisfaction with the limitations of some traditional assessment methods. The bigger issue, however, is the match between what is assessed and what the goals of learning are. For example, if learning goals include being able to transfer and apply factual knowledge to create a new product, then assessing rote factual knowledge may not be the best approach. Here the cognitive dimensions on the knowledge matrix are highly useful. The important questions to ask are: What is the cognitive process that one desires to assess?, and, what is the cognitive process embedded in the assessment? Ideally, there should be a close match. Consider the following cognitive activities and possible assessments for each:

- *Remembering*—Multiple choice, short answer
- *Understanding*—Paraphrase, describe examples
- *Applying*—Implement, perform, and use a checklist
- *Analyze*—Plan, select what is important and not important
- *Evaluate*—Apply criteria to make a judgment
- *Create*—Combine elements to invent something new and useful

Assessing the *application* of knowledge with multiple choice short answer questions would not be a good match, nor would assessing simple recall of information with procedures that require more complex processes such as *analyzing* or *evaluating* information. These examples should highlight the problems that ensue when there is a mismatch. An instructor who believes he or she was teaching complex knowledge but used rote instructional methods that encouraged only simple recall should not be surprised when students do well on recall assessments but not on those tapping higher order processes.

Considering the actual cognitive processes involved in how one will be using and assessing different kinds of knowledge helps assure that a more accurate picture of learning is created, thus leading to more effective instruction in terms of where knowledge gaps might lie.

> Considering the actual cognitive processes involved in how one will be using and assessing different kinds of knowledge helps assure that a more accurate picture of learning is created, thus leading to more effective instruction in terms of where knowledge gaps might lie.

Being Clear About Goals

The issue of goals and how they underlie the entire model considered here will be discussed in more detail in Chapter 7. Suffice it to say, however, that if those in the hierarchy of the leadership chain can't specify what those under them should know, it is a good bet that they will have unclear or contradictory understandings of what they should be doing. If people don't know what they are supposed to know, they can't achieve their goals. The knowledge matrix provides a useful tool for trying to get specific in this task.

In addition, one of the features of learners is that as they become more proficient at doing something (that is, they know more), much of their knowledge becomes *automated,* or not always consciously accessible (Alexander, 2003; Barrett, Tugade, & Engle, 2004; Clark, 2006, 2008). Consider the difference between the first time you drove a car and now (assuming you are a mature, experienced driver). Initially, every step, from inserting the key to putting the car in gear to feathering the gas while starting, to merging with traffic, and so on, requires significant concentration. Later, as expertise develops, these steps require much less effort and we think of them only momentarily or not at all. In fact, it is this feature of how knowledge is acquired and stored that allows drivers to do what they should not be doing while driving—talking on a cellphone, applying makeup, shaving, reading, and so forth. The automated nature of knowledge that is characteristic of experts sometimes makes it difficult for them to know what they know or to explain what they know to others (Feldon, 2007). Ironically, the more we know, the harder it is for us to explain to others how to do what we are good at doing! Being explicit when considering what people should know, whether student, parent, teachers, or administrators, therefore, is critical in helping them achieve important learning goals and improving performance.

> Often school debates center around what should be taught (curriculum and standards) and how it should be assessed, (which test is the best?) rather than on how to teach it.

THE INSTRUCTIONAL DIMENSION

Knowing what people should know or *how* people learn is only part of the equation. Equally important is knowing how to help them to learn. This is commonly known as the *science of instruction*. It boils down to being able to specify "which instructional methods work for teaching which kinds of knowledge to which kinds of learners under which kinds of circumstances" (Mayer, 2011, p. 3). As with many other aspects of life, it can be a deceptively simple task. It seems that often school debates center around what should be taught (curriculum and standards) and how it should be assessed, (which test is the best?) rather than on *how* to teach it. While not all theories are equal in this regard, it is also true that each provides specific tools to practitioners that will be effective under certain conditions and given certain learning goals and learner characteristics. Rather than waste time on debating the merits of the different approaches, in work with practitioners trying to solve day to day educational problems, it has proven more fruitful to consider what specific tools each provides in the service of solving learning problems. As a way of encouraging practitioners to think about how learning theory informs their work and their attempts to solve educational problems in their schools and districts, we have tried to ask the question, what does each theoretical perspective offer in the way of specific tools to improve instruction? This has evolved over time in to the creation of a toolkit that includes not only specific approaches, but also what impact they might be expected to have on learning and how it operates. Table 3.2 provides the most recent iteration of a learning toolkit.[1] Having educational practitioners create and attempt to use this toolkit has proven to be highly beneficial in not only integrating abstract theoretical ideas into practice, but in helping frame and solve specific learning

Table 3.2. A Toolkit of Instructional Methods Based on Different Approaches to Learning

Theory and Key Principles, Processes, and Concepts	Specific Learning Tools	Intended Learning Impact
Behaviorism—Focus is on observable behavior; Operant (voluntary) behavior is controlled by environmental events, respondent (involuntary) is modified by being paired with new stimuli	• Reinforcement (Premack Principle) • Extinction • Learning Objectives • Contingency Contracts • Learning hierarchies, task analysis • Pairing (UCS to CS)	• Behavior strengthened • Behavior weakened • Focuses attention & learning • Agreements to achieve objectives in return for promise of reinforcement • Insures learning of important prerequisite skills and proper sequencing of content. Most useful with structured content such as math and science, not "ill-structured" domains • For respondent behaviors, stimuli that elicit maladaptive responses can be re-conditioned (paired with an incompatible or more neutral response)
Information Processing—Focus is on internal cognitive events and processes during learning such as perception, attention, processing, storage, and recall; also takes in to account cognitive architecture such as different memory stores (working memory, short term memory, long term memory); focus on differences between novices and experts in terms of organization and store of prior knowledge, role of automaticity in performance	*Organize Information:* a. In the sequence required for recall b. In hierarchies c. In a matrix d. As a diagram • Provide integrated print and visual information about a topic—do not separate them—and do not overload learners with information *Learning Strategies:* a. Rehearsal—repeating information to be learned b. Chunking—grouping information to be remembered by category or shared qualities c. Elaboration (e.g., with analogies or examples) • Provide factual knowledge (facts) • Provide procedural knowledge *Mnemonics:* a. Key words, e.g., "Mr. Palmer" = image of palm tree; or "pluma" = image of writing with a feather pen plus pronunciation = meaning	• Improves recall by sequence, e.g., steps in a procedure • Aids hierarchical recall of structures, e.g., the periodic table • Aids matrix recall, e.g., compare and contrast goals • Aids recall of spatial relationships between units • Enhances processing time for working memory and reduces cognitive load • Helps short term retention by keeping information in working memory but largely ineffective for meaningful learning • Increases amount of information held in working memory for processing • Connects new information to similar information stored in long term memory • Learned knowledge will be conscious and available later to change or combine with new knowledge • Learned knowledge is practiced until it is automated and so does not take up working memory space • Enhances memory for definition/meaning and pronunciation of foreign language names, names of people, etc. • Enhances memory for sequence—musical chords • Enhances memory for sequence (Red, Orange, Yellow, Green, Blue, etc.)

Information Processing (*continued...*)	b. Sentence mnemonic, e.g., Every Good Boy Does Fine c. Word or acronym mnemonic, e.g., Roy G. Biv • Distributed practice • Meaningful learning—instructions to relate new information to previous experience and/or take notes that describe new information in learners' own words • Provide learning activities which encourage active not passive processing, including case-based learning • Worked examples • Encourage thinking about the "why" and "when" new information can be applied • Provide task specific feedback on performance	• Frequent practice for short periods of time helps cognitive integration of learning • Information learned meaningfully is stored more quickly and remembered more accurately because it is elaborated with prior learning • Encourages learner to connect new knowledge to prior knowledge and to construct meaning • Allows learner to apply cognitive resources to problem-relevant ("germane") demands and not extraneous demands not related to problem solution • Enhances metacognitive knowledge and transfer • Provides learner with information on how to adjust performance for improved learning
Social Cognitive Theory—focus is on reciprocal determinism, or the dynamic interactions of person (beliefs, values, attitudes, cognitions), behavior, and environmental influences; includes the role of beliefs about the self and learning tasks and activities in learning and performance	• Observational learning—modeling of to-be-learned strategies and behavior • Use of models who are credible, able to cope with problems, similar (including culture and gender appropriate), and high status • Accurate and task-specific feedback • Self-regulation	• Helps facilitate learning of complex behavioral sequences or problem solving routines • Increases the probability that the model will be imitated and the modeled strategies learned • Results in increased mental effort and persistence and attributions about the role of effort vs. ability in performance • Fosters greater learner control of behavior and cognition

Sociocultural and Sociohistorical Approaches—focuses on the role of the cultural and social bases of learning, including the role of context; includes the concept of mediation, including that provided by others in the social environment, the self, and by the cultural tools which have been inherited from past generations	• Authentic tasks—including culturally responsive instruction
	• Social interaction—cooperative learning, cognitive apprenticeships such as reciprocal teaching, and personalization methods
	• ZOPD—Target instruction to the space between a learner's level of independent performance and their level of assisted performance (Vygotsky)
	• Specific means of providing assisted performance or scaffolding:
	  a. Contingency Management
	  b. Modeling
	  c. Feedback
	  d. Questioning
	  e. Direct Instruction
	  f. Cognitive Structuring
	  g. Task Structuring
		• Tasks that are similar to those that are common to a student's familiar cultural settings promote learning and transfer
		• Facilitates construction of new knowledge
		• Assures that scaffolding and assisted performance are at the appropriate developmental level
		• Specific means of assisting the performance of a learner within his/her zone of proximal development

problems. It is surprising how many students who are themselves teachers at all levels of the educational system, from elementary school to the college level, have never really thought systematically about the specific instructional approaches they use, why they may or may not work, or how they might relate to specific types of knowledge goals.

The ability to use the tools of teaching and learning effectively, however, involves more than mastering the factual and conceptual and procedural knowledge that characterize specific tools. A danger of simply learning the *what* and *how to* but not the *why* or *when* regarding learning tools is that it leads to random hit and miss, trial and error attempts to improve instruction, or else leads to reliance on a single or small number of approaches without the ability to adapt to changing learner needs. The critical aspect is the metacognitive knowledge that allows one to decide when and why to implement a certain approach, and then when to change it in favor of something more effective. This is not a trivial matter. Many students have taken a learning course, but the vast majority report that they memorized basic facts and terms and forgot most of it when they entered the profession. The proposal here is that readers think about what they may have learned already, but in different ways, and to apply what is known in a more integrated and systematic fashion to daily problems around student learning and success.

> A danger of simply learning the *what* and *how* to but not the *why* or *when* regarding learning tools is that it leads to random hit and miss, trial and error attempts to improve instruction, or else leads to reliance on a single or small number of approaches without the ability to adapt to changing learner needs.

CHAPTER 4

The Motivational Dimension

Consider the following problems:

- Some students do not consistently attend school; others drop out of school entirely because they are not sure what they want to do
- Teachers have a hard time getting students to complete their homework
- Some students do not try hard on exams used for school accountability purposes because they don't think it is important
- Some teachers enthusiastically embrace new reform initiatives and teaching methodologies, but revert to what they were previously doing after a short period of time
- Many students choose television over reading activities in their after-school time
- When given a choice of reading materials at different levels of difficulty, some students will consistently choose challenging materials, while others will choose less challenging materials
- Teachers note that some students always put forth their best effort while others do the least amount of work possible to get by
- Some students who do not do well in school think that it is due to the fact that they are not smart
- Because of the significant changes in demographics in some schools, some teachers do not believe they have the skills to teach students who do not speak English or who are from diverse cultural backgrounds
- Some students are overly preoccupied with grades and how they do compared to other students, rather than focused on what they learned
- A principal notices that some teachers provide their students with unchallenging and low-level activities because they believe that the students do not have the ability to learn well

- Teachers believe that the principal unfairly favors some teachers over others in conducting evaluations, and therefore they do not put as much effort into their teaching as they could

What do all of these items share? They all are likely based entirely or in part on factors related to motivation. What is motivation? A quick survey of people on the street about the nature of motivation would likely result in a view that emphasizes innate factors. That is, many people tend to think of motivation as a trait that is inherent, stable, and resistant to change. In fact, some of the early work on motivation, derived from early research on animals, described motivation in terms of drives and the need for drive reduction. However, more recent work on motivation, especially what is known as achievement or academic motivation, emphasizes the beliefs that a person develops related to themselves as learners, to learning tasks and activities, and related factors to be described. It is good to keep in mind that just because someone *knows how* to do something, doesn't mean they *want* to do it or *will* do it. Moreover, it is important to keep in mind that motivational issues impact teachers, principals, and administrators just as much as they do students.

In formal terms, motivation is defined as "the process whereby goal-directed activity is instigated and sustained" (Schunk, Pintrich, & Meece, 2009, p. 4). Both the instigation and sustainment of motivation are influenced by internal (cognitive and affective) and external (social, cultural, etc.) factors, and the dynamic interplay of these two forces needs to be kept in mind. Expanding on this definition, Mayer (2011) notes that there are four critical components of motivation: it is personal (it is internal to the student), it is activating (it instigates behavior), it is energizing (fosters persistence and intensity), and it is directed (aimed at accomplishing a goal).

Schunk, Pintrich, and Meece (2009) suggest that there are three common indicators related to motivational factors: active choice, persistence, and effort. Active choice refers to deciding to choose one activity over another, persistence refers to commitment to pursue an activity over time in the face of distraction, and effort refers to the mental work needed to generate new learning and knowledge. Therefore, when people make choices, persist, or quit a task or activity, or exert effort, motivational variables are assumed to be the driving dynamic. While motivation and learning are often discussed separately, a more current view recognizes the close relationship and dynamic interplay of motivational and cognitive factors in learning.

It is true that there is fairly wide agreement about the nature of motivation; it is also true that there is not a single theory of motivation. Rather, there are various subtheories that focus on one or more of the components thought to be key aspects of motivation, and each has an extensive empirical foundation. Contemporary work on motivation has been heavily influenced by a social cognitive perspective, which describes how people form beliefs and meanings from perceptions of themselves and their environment (Bandura, 1986). While earlier conceptions of motivation largely focused on individual cognitions in motivation, increasingly, sociocultural influences such as culture and context have become increasingly important aspects of work on motivation (Graham & Hudley, 2007; Hudley & Daoud, 2007; McInerney & Van Etten, 2001, 2002; Pajares, 2007; Salili & Hoosain, 2007). It is important to keep in mind that motivation is inherently cultural. We develop motivational beliefs from others with whom we interact in the variety of social contexts in the ecological niches we inhabit.

> Motivation is inherently cultural. We develop motivational beliefs from others with whom we interact in the variety of social contexts in the ecological niches we inhabit.

A BRIEF OVERVIEW OF MOTIVATIONAL VARIABLES

A thorough review of each of the different aspects of motivation is beyond the scope of this chapter, but readers are urged to consult more detailed reviews such as Pintrich, Schunk, and Meese (2008), Wentzel and Wigfield (2009), and McInerney and Van Etten (2004). For the present purposes, it is important to understand the key dimensions that characterize motivation, nicely summarized by Pintrich (see Table 4.1). While the table specifically references students, these motivational dynamics are equally applicable to adults as well. Moreover, while the specifics of motivational beliefs will vary developmentally, culturally, and along other dimensions, the motivational principles are assumed not to vary:

- *Self-efficacy and competence beliefs*—Self-efficacy is defined as, "People's judgments of their capabilities to organize and execute the course of action required to attain designated levels of performances" (Bandura, 1986, p. 391). It is related to all three motivational indicators, and is especially important when difficulty is

Table 4.1. Motivational Principles in Action: Applications and Action Steps

Motivational Generalization	Design Principle
Adaptive self-efficacy and competence beliefs motivate students	• Provide clear and accurate feedback regarding competence and self-efficacy, focusing on the development of competence expertise, and skill • Design tasks that offer opportunities to be successful but also challenge students
Adaptive attributions and control beliefs motivate students	• Provide feedback that stresses process nature of learning, including importance of effort, strategies, and potential self-control of learning • Provide opportunities to exercise some choice and control • Build supportive and caring personal relationship in the community of learners in the classroom
Higher levels of interest and intrinsic motivation motivate students	• Provide stimulating and interesting tasks, activities, and materials, including some novelty and variety in tasks and activities • Provide content material and tasks that are personally meaningful and interesting to students • Display and model interest and involvement in the content and activities
Higher levels of value motivate students	• Provide tasks, material, and activities that are relevant and useful to students, allowing for some personal identification with school • Classroom discourse should focus on importance and utility of content and activities
Goals motivate and direct students	• Use organizational and management structures that encourage personal and social responsibility and provide a safe, comfortable, and predictable environment • Use cooperative and collaborative groups to allow for opportunities to attain both social and academic goals • Classroom discourse should focus on master learning and understanding course and lesson content • Use task, reward, and evaluation structures that promote mastery, learning, effort, progress, and self-improvement standards and less relevance on social comparison or norm-referenced standards

Note: Adapted from Pintrich, 2003

encountered while engaging in a task or activity. Competence beliefs reflect one's beliefs about his or her own ability, and are related to expectancy beliefs—that is, how well one expects to do on a task or activity. While there are important distinctions among these constructs (Schunk & Pajares, 2005), they essentially get at the question, am I able to do this task? It is important to

> Individuals with higher self-efficacy, greater belief in their own competence, and higher expectancies for positive outcomes will be more motivated to engage in, persist at, and work hard at a task or activity.

keep in mind that these constructs are different than general self-esteem, which is more focused on how one feels about oneself in general. Self-esteem is much weaker in explaining how we behave in specific tasks or activities.

These beliefs are influenced by a number of factors, including the amount of prior knowledge one has related to the task or activity, the type and amount of feedback one has received from others, as well as past successes and failures. The important motivational principle is that individuals with higher self-efficacy, greater belief in their own competence, and higher expectancies for positive outcomes will be more motivated to engage in, persist at, and work hard at a task or activity.

- *Attributions and control beliefs*—In general, attributions refer to the beliefs one has about the reasons for success or failure at a task or activity as well as the degree of control they have in affecting that outcome. Attribution theorists typically consider attributions along three dimensions—stability, locus, and control (Wiener, 2005). Stability refers to whether attributions are temporary or more permanent. It is common for low-achieving students to

> It is common for low-achieving students to believe that they lack ability or are not smart—presumably relatively permanent conditions. In contrast, attributions that focus on effort are seen as leading to different outcomes in the future.

believe that they lack ability or are not smart—presumably relatively permanent conditions. In contrast, attributions that focus on effort are unstable in the sense that they would be more amenable to change and be seen as leading to different outcomes in the future. Locus refers to whether an attribution is related to something internal to the individual or external to the individual. Arriving late for a meeting would be external if one's car had a flat tire, but neglecting to plan ahead would be internal. Internal factors are things that can be modified, while external things are usually not amenable to being modified. Finally, attributions can be categorized as things one can control (controllable) or uncontrollable. How one thinks about the unique combination of these three dimensions of attributions determines the impact on subsequent behavior, cognition, and emotions.

In attribution theory, individuals are seen as constantly trying to make sense of the larger social environment and their place within it, and attributions are part of that sense-making process. Attribution theory explains why individuals may respond differently to the same event. It leads to questions such as, "Why did I fail that exam?" or "Why am I having such a hard time engaging students in the lessons I prepare?" or "Why am I unable to provide effective leadership to my teachers around this new curriculum initiative?" Note that it is not necessary that attributions be accurate for them to have behavioral consequences. From a motivational perspective, attributions largely address the questions, "Why did I succeed or fail at this task?" and "Is there something I can do to improve my performance next time?" The important motivational principle is that when an individual believes that failing to meet a goal is not necessarily permanent and can be influenced by things that can be controlled, such as increased effort, they are likely to be choose, persist, and work hard at a task or activity.

- *Value*—In general, value (or task value, as it is often called in the motivation literature) refers to the importance one attaches to a task. It gets at the question, "Why should I do this task?" A useful perspective on task value is provided by Wigfield and Eccles (2000, 2002). They consider four separate dimensions of task value: attainment or importance value, intrinsic value, utility value, and cost value. Attainment value refers to the importance one attaches to doing well on a task. Note that there are a variety of reasons why one might have high attainment value. Intrinsic value refers to the enjoyment or intrinsic interest one experiences in a particular activity. Utility value refers to how useful one believes a task or activity is for achieving some future goal. Finally, cost value is the perceived cost of the activity in terms of time, effort, or other dimensions. It is the dynamic interaction around the beliefs in these four dimensions that is assumed to determine the overall value one attaches to a task. While going to medical school is known to have a high cost value (financial, time, effort), this might be overshadowed by the attainment, intrinsic, and perceived utility of achieving the larger career goal of completing a prestigious degree, financial reward, and increased ability to help individuals. The important motivational principle

> Sometimes people give up on trying to achieve their goals simply because they are too vague, they don't know how to make progress in achieving them, or the goal is too difficult to tackle all at once.

is that the higher an individual values an activity, the more likely he or she chooses, persists, and engages in it. Values are most influential in starting an activity, while expectancies are most influential in persisting at an activity (National Research Council, 2004).

- *Goals*—Simply stated, a goal is "something that the person wants to achieve" (Locke & Latham, 1990, p. 2). There are two different ways that goals are considered in the motivation literature. One is known as *goal content* and the other focuses on *goal orientation*. The work on goal content is heavily based on social cognitive theory (Bandura, 2001), and the role of goals in motivating behavior; and focuses on characteristics of goals such as whether they are current (proximal), concrete (specific), and challenging (Locke & Latham, 2002). Sometimes people give up trying to achieve their goals simply because the goals are too vague, they don't know how to make progress in achieving them, or the goal is too difficult to tackle all at once. Goal content gets at the question, "What is it that I want?" While there is work on a variety of different types of goals, such as social goals (Wentzel, 2000), and individuals can and do pursue multiple goals simultaneously, the general assumption is that when multiple goals are aligned and not in conflict, they are likely to lead to more adaptive behavior than when they are not.

- The motivational literature also describes goals in terms of *goal orientations*. Originally developed to explain school-based learning, it is a perspective that focuses more on the purposes or reasons for engaging in achievement behaviors (Pintrich, 2003). In more specific terms, goal orientation is defined as a pattern of beliefs that represent "different ways of approaching, engaging in, and responding to achievement situations" (Ames, 1992, p. 261). While there are various approaches to goal orientations, goal orientation theorists normally distinguish between a *mastery goal orientation* and a *performance goal orientation*. In general, a mastery goal orientation leads one to approach a task in order to learn, gain new competence, accomplish a challenging activity, and so forth. A performance goal orientation, on the other hand, leads one to focus more on demonstrating ability in front of others, on seeking rewards or recognition, on besting others, and avoiding others' negative judgments about low ability. Further, each of these goal orientations can lead either to *approach* or *avoid* a task.

When intersected, these dimensions result in a 2 x 2 matrix. At first glance, it might appear that a mastery performance is the ideal target. Most teachers are thrilled when they have students who seem to be interested in learning for its own sake, and who actively and constantly seek to learn more. Conversely, many teachers are less satisfied with students who seem to be only motivated and obsessed by grades and by looking better than others, irrespective of what they learn. While much of the initial work on goal orientations focused on the positive aspects of a mastery goal orientation and its relation to achievement and other outcomes, more recent views have tended to downplay the good/bad dichotomy with the realization that some performance-oriented students actually achieve well, and that a performance orientation may actually be adaptive in some situations, especially in situations (athletics comes to mind) where competition and ranking are valued (Elliot, 2006). What does appear to have negative consequences is the avoidance pattern, especially when paired with a performance goal orientation.

> Motivational beliefs and processes are context-specific, so for example a student can have very different self-efficacy beliefs in one subject and not another, or even on two different activities within the same classroom.

For the purposes of this chapter, it is important to keep in mind how these factors can influence the functioning of districts, schools, and classrooms, as well as the individuals that inhabit them. It should be remembered that these motivational beliefs and processes are context-specific, so for example, a student can have very different self-efficacy beliefs in one subject and not another, or even on two different activities within the same classroom. It is also important to keep in mind that motivation is normally directed toward a particular goal, sometimes known only to the individual. When a teacher says that a particular student is not motivated, it is possible that the

> When a teacher says that a particular student is not motivated, it is possible that the student is not motivated with respect to the goal that the teacher has in mind but toward an entirely different goal.

student is not motivated with respect to the goal that the teacher has in mind but toward an entirely different goal. In the course of a recent study (Monzo & Rueda, 2009), for example, we were doing classroom observations of elementary-level students who were in the process of acquiring English. In this particular school and community context, a very high value was placed on speaking English as well as reading and writing in English. We noted that many students often created distractions during round robin reading, or when called on by the teacher to answer reading comprehension would say "I don't know" or give any made-up answer. Since we knew these students were normally competent and otherwise well-behaved, we were puzzled by their behavior. It eventually came to light through conversations in Spanish that the students were not oriented toward the seemingly obvious goal of displaying their knowledge, but rather toward the goal of *masking their inability to understand or perform in English.* Their disruptions and careless or incorrect answers were not simple mistakes, they were conscious strategies employed toward the goal of feigning competence in English. While they were *not* engaged in the teacher's goal of promoting literacy skills, they *were* quite engaged in their own goal of maintaining the appearance of competence. This goal, of course, was heavily influenced by the strong pressure in this school to be English-fluent at all costs, and the negative social sanctions associated with being a non-English speaker.

> It eventually came to light through conversations in Spanish that the students were not oriented toward the seemingly obvious goal of displaying their knowledge, but rather toward the goal of masking their inability to understand or perform in English. Their disruptions and careless or incorrect answers were not simple mistakes, they were conscious strategies employed toward the goal of feigning competence in English.

MOTIVATIONAL FACTORS IN PRACTICE

How do the motivation factors just reviewed facilitate or impede institutional or individual goals? Consider this for a moment: The sociocultural context can influence motivation in a variety of ways. Think of the ways that teachers can have an impact on student performance by the following, for example:

- Giving some students less time to answer a question than others
- Giving students answers, or calling on others rather than trying to improve their responses by giving clues or rephrasing questions
- Reinforcing inappropriately; rewarding their inappropriate behavior or incorrect answers
- Criticizing them more often for failure
- Praising them less frequently than high achievers for success
- Paying less attention to them or interacting with them less frequently
- Calling on them less often
- Seating them at a distance from the teacher
- Demanding less from them
- Giving feedback that focuses on student deficits rather than on how to improve and be successful on a task
- Providing positive feedback even when an answer or problem solution is wrong

Epstein (1989) identified at least six different ways that the social and physical organization of a classroom can affect motivation, including task design, distribution of authority, recognition of students, grouping arrangements, evaluation practices, and time allocation. The acronym for these factors is TARGET, derived from the first letter of the relevant aspect—(task, authority, recognition, grouping, evaluation, and time). Clearly, there are a myriad of ways that teacher, classroom, and school factors can impact how and whether students engage or not.

> Epstein (1989) identified at least six different ways that the social and physical organization of a classroom can affect motivation, including task design, distribution of authority, recognition of students, grouping arrangements, evaluation practices, and time allocation.

Now think about how motivational factors for teachers might be influenced by a school setting where:

- The goals of the school are not clear
- The goals are constantly changing with no discernable reason
- The goals seem arbitrary and imposed with no input from those who are expected to implement them
- There is a constant lack of resources and dilapidated working conditions
- Public perceptions of teachers in general are overwhelmingly negative
- The range of student ethnic, racial, linguistic, and cultural backgrounds in the classroom have increased significantly, but no specialized professional development or other resources are available
- Rewards and teaching assignments are determined based on seniority rather than on hard work or other indicators of teaching excellence
- There is a constant influx of new innovations that are embraced and then seem to be disregarded by administrators after a short period of time in favor of the next new thing
- There is a constant threat of layoffs because of budgetary constraints, and moreover these are based on seniority rather than success as a teacher
- It is difficult to uphold behavioral or academic standards because administrators are overly sensitive to political rather than educational considerations and do not support teachers when students or parents complain

While the specifics are expected to vary, the motivational dynamics and principles that apply to students apply equally to the adults in school settings. What is surprising is how infrequently the motivational dimensions of performance problems and issues are systematically considered in most school settings. Most often, the causes of performance issues are assumed to be gaps in what people know—and a new curriculum, new professional development, or new training is instituted. Rarely is consideration given to the possibility that individuals actually *do* know what they are supposed to be doing, but *choose not to*

> Motivational dynamics and principles that apply to students apply equally to the adults in school settings.

> Motivational problems are not solved by solutions that are designed to address knowledge gaps.

do it. The importance in making this distinction is that *motivational problems are not solved by solutions that are designed to address knowledge gaps.* Moreover, motivation issues can be due to a variety of causes, and should not be seen as a one-dimensional phenomenon. Solutions designed to address one type of motivational problem (for example, self-efficacy) will likely not solve other types of motivational problems (task value). In addition to this caution, two other points are worth keeping in mind. First, motivational beliefs are likely to be context-specific, so that motivational causes should be considered with respect to the dynamics of specific situations. Second, it is not *actual* events or conditions that are most relevant for individual motivation, but rather *perceived* conditions or events. Thus two people experiencing the identical conditions or events can have very different perceptions with resulting motivational consequences.

ASSESSING AND ADDRESSING
MOTIVATIONAL ISSUES

Motivational constructs can be assessed in a variety of ways, although the research literature has most often relied on self-report measures, including self-rating scales. These have the advantage, if carefully constructed, of allowing quantifying otherwise abstract constructs. They also have the disadvantage of relying on individuals to validly and reliably report on their own motivational beliefs and processes. Outside of a research context, for example, while trying to solve performance problems in educational settings, it is possible to draw on a range of approaches including interviews, informal conversations, focus groups, and careful observation.

How are motivation issues best solved? A thorough answer could take volumes, and many motivation researchers spend entire careers on a single aspect of motivation. However, a working knowledge of basic motivational constructs and principles can be a powerful tool in diagnosing and solving many motivational issues. Table 4.1 provides some approaches for specific motivational problems. These are useful, but it will be noted that they

> Working knowledge of basic motivational constructs and principles can be a powerful tool in diagnosing and solving many motivational issues.

are general in nature, and skewed toward solving achievement-related issues with students (for an organizational perspective, see Clark, 2005). In addition, they may represent a case of easier said than done. For example, consider the expertise required to provide clear and accurate feedback or to provide stimulating and interesting tasks. These really get at the foundations of what is required to be a highly qualified and effective teacher (or administrator). They do provide important guidance and allow a useful and concrete starting point from which context-specific and meaningful solutions can be created based on existing expertise and knowledge of the local context.

UNRESOLVED ISSUES

The understanding of motivation has increased substantially over the last couple of decades. However, a word of caution is in order. As noted earlier, there is no overarching theory that encompasses the range of motivational constructs. There is not always agreement in the literature about the definition or measurement of specific constructs. There is not always clear differentiation of motivational constructs with related constructs such as *engagement* or *emotions* (Pekrun, 2007). Too often the environment-motivation-learning connections are considered as linear and unidirectional rather than as dynamic and interactive, and the role of conscious versus unconscious processes in motivation is only beginning to be explored (Immordino-Yang & Sylvan, in press). In spite of these limitations, there is little doubt that an understanding of motivation provides a powerful set of tools in helping schools address performance problems at a variety of levels.

> Understanding of motivation provides a powerful set of tools in helping schools address performance problems.

CHAPTER 5

The Organizational Dimension

Consider the following issues:

- Schools are asked to do more with fewer resources
- *Best practice* calls for the integration of special and regular education in order to provide more coherent and effective programs—but teacher education programs are separate, as are professional development activities for special education and other teachers
- Accountability requirements mandate that schools be evaluated on normative measures that compare them to others—so that even though they don't achieve at the "norm" and did make progress during a given time period they are still penalized
- The newest teachers are assigned to the students who require the most assistance
- Bullying is tolerated except when outside attention is focused on the problem
- Diversity among students is seen as a problem to be addressed within the school
- There are inadequate mechanisms in place to mentor new teachers
- Principals are so immersed in paperwork and bureaucratic requirements that they are unable to provide instructional leadership
- Athletes and popular students are penalized less or not at all for the same transgressions that result in harsher consequences for other students
- Some schools see parents as the enemy and other schools see them as collaborators

It sometimes happens that even when everyone in a specific school or work setting knows what, when, and why they are supposed to do something to achieve the organizations' goals, and even when they are highly

> Athletes and popular students are penalized less or not at all for the same transgressions that result in harsher consequences for other students.

motivated to do so, there are things about the organization itself that impede their performance. These organizational features include how the setting is structured and organized, the policies and practices that define it, and even how people interact with each other within the setting. These features are important because there is evidence that aspects of educational settings, such as the quality and frequency of teacher-student interaction (Lundberg & Schreiner, 2004), or students' perceptions of things such as institutional barriers (Kenny, Blustein, Chaves, Grossman, & Gallagher, 2003), can be factors in successful student outcomes, and can have far-reaching effects on how people behave and think in those settings.

> Aspects of educational settings, such as the quality and frequency of teacher-student interaction (Lundberg & Schreiner, 2004), or students' perceptions of things such as institutional barriers (Kenny, Blustein, Chaves, Grossman, & Gallagher, 2003), can be factors in successful student outcomes, and can have far-reaching effects on how people behave and think.

ARE POOR LEADERS TO BLAME?

A recent book on leadership, *When Leadership Goes Wrong: Destructive Leadership, Mistakes, and Ethical Failures* (Schyns & Hansbrough, 2010) addressed this question. A quick view of some of the major section headings of the volume provides a flavor of the content: Destructive Leaders; Abusive Supervision; Toxic Leadership, Narcissism, and (un-) Ethical Leadership; and Leader Errors and Failures. Many readers may have worked in a setting with a boss, supervisor, or administrator who they think is a perfect fit for one or more of these descriptors. You might recall what impact this may have had on your own behavior, thoughts, and attitudes during the time you were in that setting. Yet there are organizational factors other than incompetent administrators that can facilitate or impede the achievement of both individual and organizational goals. Administrators and supervisors may be an easy target, but the reality is a bit more complex.

There are a variety of approaches that suggest that organizational factors are important to consider in school outcomes and discussions of student achievement. In areas outside of K–12 education, there has been

considerable attention devoted to how organizations function and how they change over time. In
the higher education and business literature, for example, the notion of *organizational learning* is promi-
nent (Chance, 2009; Kezar, 2005). Simply described,
organizational learning refers to the ways in which
organizations (as opposed to individuals) learn and
adapt to challenges and changes in the environ-

> Administrators and supervisors may be an easy target, but the reality is a bit more complex.

ment. Although this perspective has only rarely been applied to K–12 settings (Imants, 2003), (which are the focus of this book), it does offer an
interesting way to think about how schools function as an organization
rather than as a simple collection of individuals.

Other approaches that look at organizational factors are based on
organizational theories with roots in sociology, industrial and organizational psychology, sociocultural theories related to culture and context,
and even work related to school reform and restructuring. All of these approaches have a different emphasis. However, they are united in making
the point that organizations and institutions can be a major influence on
performance goals. Thus, in addition to considering how knowledge gaps
and motivation gaps can impact the attainment of goals, it is necessary to
look at the third component, organizational gaps.

THE ROOTS OF ORGANIZATIONAL GAPS

In thinking about organizations for our purposes, it is useful to consider
the areas of culture, structure, and policies and practices. Although classrooms, schools, and districts are unique in many ways, these areas are just
as important to attaining goals as they would be for any other organization. As Thacker, Bell, and Schargel (2009, p. 6) note, schools and educational organizations:

- Are complex systems in which one part of the system is tied to
  another
- Have structures that have been built by scaffolding one structure
  onto another over time
- Unlike other systems, have more emotional strings attached because the well- being of children is inextricably tied to the success
  or failure of the systems.

> Much of what we consider cultural knowledge is *automated,* and therefore not always transparent or easily accessible.

It is worth taking a more detailed look at the specific organizational features that will be considered in our analysis of organizational gaps. These include organizational culture, structure, policies, and practices. The notions of *cultural models* and *cultural settings* will be introduced to help make these ideas a bit more concrete. The next section will first describe organizational culture followed by a brief discussion of organizational structures.

Organizational Culture

Culture and cultural processes, which are often thought of as pertaining to individuals rather than organizations, are notoriously difficult to define and operationalize for several reasons: 1. they are not always visible; 2. much of what we consider cultural knowledge is *automated*, and therefore not always transparent or easily accessible to individuals or individuals within a specific organizational setting; and 3. they involve values that are relative. There is not complete agreement about the definition of culture or what the key aspects are. Nevertheless, culture and cultural processes can be used to describe not only individuals, but organizations as well.

Schein (2004a), in discussing organizational culture, has noted that all of the following have been used at some point to describe culture: observed behavioral regularities when people interact; group norms; espoused values; formal philosophy; rules of the game; climate; embedded skills; habits of thinking, mental models, and linguistic paradigms; shared meanings; *root metaphors,* or integrating symbols; and formal rituals and celebrations. Culture is often mistakenly used interchangeably with group labels related to race or ethnicity. Thus, specifying that an individual is Asian is assumed to say something about that person's culture. Other unfortunate practices when considering culture include focusing on surface features of culture, such as dress or food preferences, or assuming that cultural influences operate rigidly in all settings. As Gutierrez and Rogoff (2003) caution, however, culture should not be seen as static nor monolithic, but as a dynamic process that is jointly created by individuals in

> Culture should not be seen as static or monolithic, but as a dynamic process that is jointly created and re-created by individuals in the course of negotiating everyday life.

the course of negotiating everyday life. Thus, we are not born with culture, but rather it is dynamic and continually created and re-created in the course of daily life.

A useful discussion of culture and cultural processes is found in Gallimore and Goldenberg (2001), who introduce the notion of *cultural models*. Basically, cultural models are the shared mental schema or normative understandings of how the world works, or ought to work. Cultural models can be used to characterize organizations, business settings, and classrooms, as well as individuals. Cultural models are dynamic rather than static traits, and are expressed through cultural practices (behavior, artifacts, rules, etc.) in specific contexts. Gallimore and Goldenberg (2001) suggest that these processes "represent, in a given community or ecological niche, historically evolved and shared ways of perceiving, thinking, and storing possible responses to adaptive challenges and changing conditions. Cultural models are so familiar they are often invisible and unnoticed by those who hold them" (p. 47). While Gallimore and Goldenberg discussed cultural models with respect to individuals, they are equally helpful in thinking about schools and other organizations.

Within a school or organizational setting, cultural models help shape the ways that an organization is structured, including the values, practices, policies, reward structures, and so forth.

A good overview of the notion of culture, the various ways that it has been treated in the literature, and its application to organizational and work settings is found in Schein (2004b). He defines it as:

> a pattern of shared basic assumptions that was learned by a group as it solved its problems of external adaptation and internal integration, that has worked well enough to be considered valid and, therefore, to be taught to new members as the correct way to perceive, think, and feel in relation to those problems (p. 17).

It often helps explain why sometimes seemingly unreasonable behavior or thinking makes sense in a specific context. Which administrator or supervisor has not encountered the following dilemma expressed so well by Schein (2004b)?

> As managers, when we try to change the behavior of subordinates, we often encounter resistance to change to an extent that seems beyond reason. We observe departments in our organization that seem to be more interested in fighting with each other than getting the job done. We

> see communication problems and misunderstandings between group members that should not be occurring between reasonable people. We explain in detail why something different must be done, yet people continue to act as if they had not heard us. (p. 9)

While the preceding quote illustrates a common concern for administrators, one can also ask about the experiences of those in schools who have been on the receiving end of various innovation and reform efforts or reorganization initiatives. From the perspective of either the giver or the receiver, the experience of trying to change organizational behavior and thinking can be equally baffling or frustrating. The annals of the school reform literature are replete with examples of how new and promising innovations get ignored, implemented partially or unevenly, or turn in to *lethal mutations* (to borrow a term from biology) that bear little resemblance to the original idea. Yet often it is possible to gain a deeper understanding of the dynamics of a given context, which in turn makes seemingly nonsensical, destructive, aggressive, or irrational thinking and behavior appear to be more rational. Such understanding can also help explain how and why these types of behavior or attitudes developed, and thus how they might be channeled in a more productive fashion. Schools, like any other context involving humans, are not neutral or blank canvasses to be painted upon; rather change takes place as an interaction of the new and the existing. As will be reiterated later in the chapter, the important point to keep in mind regarding cultural models either of individuals, or an entire school, or organization is how they promote or impede the goals that are being pursued. Understanding what these cultural models are is the first important step in tackling this issue, and if they are found to be barriers to achieving key goals, they can be an important focus for targeted solutions.

> The annals of the school reform literature are replete with examples of how new and promising innovations get ignored, implemented partially or unevenly, or turn into *lethal mutations.*

> Schools, like any other context involving humans, are not neutral or blank canvasses to be painted upon; rather change takes place as an interaction of the new and the existing.

Organizational Structure, Practices, and Policies

While organizations are characterized by cultural models, they are also made up of various social contexts (cultural settings) where organizational policies and practices are enacted. While cultural models help gain some understanding of the invisible aspects of schools and other educational and organizational work settings, Gallimore & Goldenberg's (2001) notion of *cultural settings* can be helpful in thinking about the more visible aspects. As these authors note,

> A complex social context such as a classroom, therefore, would be made up of a myriad of dynamic and changing cultural settings.

cultural models help define what is customary and normal. However, it is in specific work settings—classrooms, meeting places, playgrounds, administrator's offices, cafeterias, teacher lunch rooms, and so forth, where those models develop, and where they are played out. Thus, it is important to consider the features of specific contexts where behavior is enacted.

Cultural settings can be seen as the who, what, when, where, why, and how of the routines which constitute everyday life—in essence, a more concrete version of what we commonly call a social context (Cole, 1996; Engeström, Miettinen, & Punamäki, 1999; Tharp & Gallimore, 1988). Any time one or more of these defining features changes, then it can be considered as a new social context or cultural setting. A complex social context such as a classroom, therefore, would be made up of a myriad of dynamic and changing cultural settings. As sociocultural theorists (Kozulin, Gindis, Ageyez, & Miller, 2003; Rogoff, 2003) remind us, behavior and social context are highly intertwined. In trying to understand and perhaps influence behavior and/or thought in a classroom, school, or district, it is important to understand the characteristics of the cultural settings that make up that entity.

> In trying to understand and perhaps influence behavior and/or thought in a classroom, school, or district, it is important to understand the characteristics of the cultural settings that make up that entity.

The Reciprocal Relationships of Cultural Models and Settings

While cultural settings can impact behavior, cultural settings are also shaped by individuals and groups—who operate with cultural models that impact their own behavior. One way that cultural settings come to be what they are is through the actions of the people who inhabit them. Thus, the reciprocal relationships between cultural models and cultural settings are best thought of not as mechanistic and static in nature, but rather as dynamic and interactional processes.

A noneducational example of how these features are dynamically intertwined can be seen in the way that the smoking habit is viewed today in comparison to 20 or 30 years ago, where the differences are enormous. In earlier times, smoking was seen as glamorous or at most an innocuous habit. However, with increased public education, greater awareness of health education, and other factors, smoking is now seen as dangerous to the individual as well as a threat to others. Smoking was freely done in any setting in earlier times. Yet ideas about smoking began to shape new cultural settings, for example, the creation of "smoking only" sections of airplanes, restaurants, and so forth. As ideas (cultural models about what is appropriate, healthy, etc.) have come to shift even more, measures that are more stringent have been implemented, including the outright banning of smoking in any enclosed space, especially around children, and even in open spaces such as beaches (cultural setting norms). The significance of this change is not always readily seen, but can become apparent by considering other social contexts, for example, visiting countries where smoking is still seen as an innocuous habit. Thus, the cultural models and cultural settings influence each other and change over time in interactive ways. The examples at the beginning of the chapter provide a small window into how cultural models and settings can and do operate in educational settings. These types of processes help describe the differences that one might experience and observe while visiting different schools. The cultural artifacts that are displayed, for example, might include scholastic honors in one place, versus athletic honors in another. Likewise, one school might have an almost prisonlike feel, complete with guards, security checkpoints, and gated enclosures with locks and chains, while another school in the same community can feel much more like a welcoming community center. One school might welcome cultural and linguistic diversity while another puts policies and practices in place that actively discourage it. All of these types of cultural setting variations represent organizational characteristics that were not mandated by some external entity; rather they develop and are created by individuals and groups over time.

Understanding the genesis of these organizational factors helps explain, in part, how schools, classrooms, and other educational institutions are structured differently, why certain policies and rules exist, why certain things may get sanctioned in one place and rewarded in another, and why people may be pushed to behaving in one way as opposed to another. People often speak of learning "the lay of the land" when talking about starting a new position in an unfamiliar place. It really means gaining familiarity with the cultural models and settings in that site. These organizational structures, policies, and practices are of interest to us because they can influence whether the performance goals of individuals, groups, or entire schools or or-

> Organizational structures, policies, and practices can influence whether the performance goals of individuals, groups, or entire schools or organizational units are met.

ganizational units are met. Simply stated, organizational structures and policies, as they get instantiated in various cultural settings, can be a hindrance to improved performance and meeting goals, even when people are knowledgeable and motivated to achieve those goals.

An Example of an Organizational Gap: English Learner Referrals to Special Education

An example of how these factors can operate in practice is taken from work I was doing at an elementary school several years ago. The issue I and my colleagues were examining at this school was the high rate of special education referrals of English Learner students who were already in bilingual classrooms. At first, we believed that there was a knowledge gap and that teachers did not have sufficient professional development about the special education criteria or about how to teach in bilingual settings. We also thought the high referral rate might be due to motivational gaps, for example having low expectations of students or not wanting to deal with so called low-performing students. Upon closer investigation, we found that these factors were not in fact problems. Rather, teachers told us that there was a policy in place that when students were placed in one program (e.g., a bilingual program) they were no longer eligible for services for other programs (special intervention programs or services). The teachers indicated that some students needed additional help that they could not provide, given the large numbers of students in their classes and other demands. They stated that they clearly knew that many of the referrals were inappropriate, but that the only way to get students more individualized attention and additional assistance was to refer them for special education. These teachers had sufficient knowledge and motivation to make appropriate referrals, but a school policy caused them to act in a way that would be considered dysfunctional without a clearer understanding of the situation. Sometimes the dysfunction lies not in individual knowledge gaps or motivation issues, but in organizational structures or policies that are counterproductive.

An Example of an Organizational Gap: The Principal as Instructional Leader

In one elementary school, I and my colleagues conducted a research project related to motivation and literacy (Monzo & Rueda, 2000). A major focus of the study was students' motivational characteristics in different types of classroom activities. We interviewed the principal regarding her perspective on instructional practices affecting English Learner students, and her role as an instructional leader within the school. This particular school was in the skid-row area of the central city, and was almost exclusively populated by Latino students, many of whom were non-English speaking. In addition, a large number of students in the school were homeless or lived in cheap downtown hotels. The instructional needs of these students were significant.

Ideally, as the educational literature would suggest (Glatthorn & Jailall, 2009; Zepeda, 2007), the principal acts as an instructional leader for the school. While it is clear that these instructional responsibilities have to be balanced with the administrative requirements of making sure that a school runs smoothly and efficiently, sometimes an optimal balance is difficult to achieve. At this school, the administrative demands were excessive. This was due in part to the fact that over the years, wave after wave of new mandated programs and reforms and initiatives were introduced to the school by the central district office—while few if any were ever removed. Thus, there was somewhat of a layered effect that was evident when the principal showed us a two-and-a-half page list of the mandated programs and projects over which she currently had administrative responsibility. Each new initiative that was introduced did not replace an existing one; rather it was added to the list, often

> Over the years, wave after wave of new mandated programs and reforms and initiatives were introduced to the school by the central district office—while few if any were ever removed. Thus, there was somewhat of a layered effect.

requiring district-led training regarding implementation and administration of the new initiative.

In addition to these district requirements, a highly bureaucratic and inefficient central district office made seemingly simple administrative tasks difficult and time-consuming. In order to change a light bulb, for example, or make a simple repair to a heater or air conditioner, a special form had to be filled out and sent to the central office where it had to be processed and then placed in the queue until such time as the person providing the service was sent by the district. Sometimes the needed work was simple enough to be addressed by the custodian already at the school, but union regulations did not permit anyone other than a unionized district repairman to do the work. What should have been a simple matter became both time-consuming and inefficient, impairing the ability of the principal to address instructional matters.

Finally, while many teachers were exceedingly hard-working and put in many extra hours, other teachers were committed to doing the bare minimum. Because of union requirements, it was very difficult if not impossible to require problematic teachers to do anything that might be seen as outside of the very specific requirements of the job. Thus, training or other opportunities typically were not utilized by those who needed the most professional development. Because of these and other organizational constraints, the principal found it impossible to provide instructional leadership that was so desperately needed.

Do Organizational Gaps Exist Only in K–12 Schools?

These types of organizational impediments to performance are not confined to K–12 schools. They are characteristic to some extent of virtually any organization inside or outside of education. At my own university, faculty commonly complain about the fact that the navigation of the bureaucracy necessary to apply for and manage a research grant is harder than actually conceiving the ideas and securing the funding to carry out the work. Sometimes the policies and structures are in place for good reason, such as the need to have a review process to assure the protection of human subjects and ethical behavior in carrying out and disseminating research. However, it is also true that sometimes these bureaucratic policies and practices exist for reasons that have little to do with actually improving the quality or the work or safeguarding the rights of participants.

Changing Cultural Models and Settings:
The Case of the University of Southern California

It is natural to wonder what is involved in changing the cultural models and settings in an educational setting. A good illustration comes from my own university, where the Rossier School of Education has witnessed a significant transformation over the last decade. This example is not meant to suggest that universities and K–12 schools are interchangeable; it is very obvious that there are significant differences between K–12 schools and universities. However, the example does provide a look at how the factors described in this chapter operate in a real-world setting; while the setting is not a K–12 school or district, the principles and lessons learned remain relevant.

The Rossier School's transformation took place in a context similar in some ways to public K–12 schools that find themselves in disarray due to low student and teacher morale, isolated faculty, budgeting unpredictability, confusing requirements, program proliferation, insufficient and inconsistent student advising, and unmet student academic and other needs. For many public schools, the mandate to dissolve and reconstitute themselves comes from external sources that judge the school's test scores and insufficient annual yearly progress as evidence to require their reconstruction. In the Rossier School's case, while the mandate to change was technically voluntary, there was strong pressure from the university to make major changes in order to raise the quality and rankings of the school.

In the case of the Rossier School (prior to its restructuring beginning in 2000), meeting students' needs had come to be seen as a necessary burden by many faculty. The school was organized in ways that were more based on faculty needs than student needs. For example, there was little centralization of class schedules, and scheduling tended to be driven by faculty's preferred teaching times and days. Thus, many required courses were scheduled at the same time, creating a big problem for students. Many faculty members were unwilling to give up their favored specialization or courses they had taught for years. There was a proliferation of courses and one-faculty member degree specializations with varying schedules and requirements pertaining to each individual specialization. The curriculum was largely based on what faculty members wanted to teach, rather than a careful analysis of student career needs. The idiosyncratic and constantly changing requirements were confusing for students, and even for many faculty members. As noted earlier, there was little distinction between the professional doctorate (Ed.D.) and the Ph.D. degree other than perceived status, since much of the coursework over-lapped, and equal numbers of students in each degree program were ad-mitted. An additional problem was that in many specializations, students could take courses in any sequence, with no fixed schedule. Therefore, enrollments in any given course or specialization area fluctuated, some-times dramatically, from semester to semester. The idiosyncratic nature of the requirements and the sheer number of courses and program op-tions, in addition to the consequences already mentioned, also resulted in the school's inability to forecast enrollments even one semester into the future. Almost every year this resulted in budget chaos, since school revenues are highly dependent on tuition. This budget instability con-tinually put the school in conflict with the central administration, which emphasized accurate revenue forecasts, long-range projections, and bal-anced budgets for all academic units.

In addition to the fiscal problems, the only support for students in terms of advising or other types of academic assistance came from indi-vidual faculty members, if the faculty had time. The record-keeping and paperwork requirements mostly fell to faculty, and given the lack of effi-cient systems in place, and lack of support services, there were often prob-lems with accuracy and lost paperwork. There were few ways for students to establish or maintain a connection to the school since the courses were offered in the very late afternoon or evening to accommodate schedules of our students who are primarily working school administrators; and there were few, if any, organized activities out of class. Morale was often low on the part of faculty. There was little agreement or clarity on the mission of the school or what made it unique or distinctive, and a great degree of unevenness in what students learned. Faculty tended to be isolated within departments, with little scholarly contact among faculty from different de-partments. An external evaluation of the school suggested that it was not achieving its goals and that changes needed to be made.

It was recognized that major organizational changes were necessary. A schoolwide 3-day conference was held, with the primary goal to create a new direction for the Rossier School and to overcome its problems. One of the first steps was to recognize what the organizational problems were that were impacting the goal of becoming a highly-ranked university. In support of the change process, one of the first tasks was to come to agree-ment about the mission of the school. This was accomplished in part by examining the most pressing educational and social problems presented by public education. Given the complex challenges in urban schools, agreement was reached that the focus of the school would be leadership in urban education, with the professional doctorate (Ed.D.) as the flagship degree. To support this goal and mission, four themes were adopted that would provide levers for professional practice: leadership, diversity, accountability, and learning. Teams of faculty worked intensively on new courses, requirements, and other features of the program, starting with an analysis of who the students were and what their needs would require in their urban school settings. As a result of the planning process, specific changes were adopted which, again, can be seen to have direct corollaries to changes that are often needed to strengthen performance in K–12 settings:

- *Curriculum coherence:* Four core courses were developed to mirror the new themes and to specifically address the urban school leadership needs of students. Courses were developed by applying a *reverse engineering* approach—starting with the end goals in mind and working backward.
- *A commitment to addressing student needs:* A strong commitment to meeting student needs and making the program student friendly, more efficient, and effective was embraced—staff who had problems in these areas were not continued.
- *Providing autonomy with limits:* Program options were significantly modified so that all students took the same four courses, and then had a limited selection (four) of concentration options to select from.
- *Making structural changes to support organizational goals:* A limited number of concentrations were created to mirror students' eventual career paths and interests—these currently include K–12 leadership in urban school settings, educational psychology, higher education administration, and teacher education in multicultural societies. The number of courses was limited by agreement, and teams of faculty worked to develop the courses in each specialization—with a strong focus on relevance for practitioners and application of course material to K–12 settings.
- *Making an impact on the field:* The size of the Ed.D. program was significantly increased, with a goal of producing leaders in urban education in sufficient numbers to make a difference.
- *Shifting resources to match priorities and goals:* The size of the Ph.D.

program was significantly reduced, with a focus on preparing students for research and teaching careers in major research universities.

- *Providing adequate resources to accomplish goals:* New support offices were created with a director and dedicated advisors for each program.
- *Monitoring student performance proactively:* An Early Warning System, used by all faculty teaching core courses, was designed as a proactive measure to identify and provide assistance to students with academic difficulties in the very first year of the program.
- *Providing academic support where needed:* A Support Center was created specifically to assist students with writing issues, as well as with more general topics such as study strategies, anxiety control, and so forth.
- *Recognizing the social nature of learning:* The program adopted a cohort model that allowed students to form professional and social bonds during the program.
- *Reducing organizational barriers to collaboration:* The existing academic departments were eliminated—and the school was reorganized around programs (Ed.D., Ph.D., Masters). Faculty-led steering committees were put in place to provide governance over each of the degree programs.
- *Promote individual ownership of organizational goals:* All faculty were considered to be Ed.D. faculty (although most faculty work in at least one other program), such that the Ed.D. program was school-wide, rather than isolated in a single academic department as in many other places.
- *Making curriculum and activities relevant:* Collaboration and relevance were emphasized. The norm for dissertation work shifted from individual dissertations to group dissertations with a strong practitioner focus. Individual dissertations focused on theoretical issues gave way to teams of students who, although they still produced individual products, worked on applied problems and collaborated in ways similar to real-world practice.
- *Tailor organizational structures to meet different goals.* There is now a clear separation of the Ed.D. and Ph.D. programs, and students and faculty alike are able to articulate what those differences are— the major difference is no longer simply one of prestige or status, but rather students' career goals.

While these steps should not be taken as an exact road map to follow in a rigid fashion when organizational gaps are being addressed, taken as a whole, they do offer some important strategies for helping to close these gaps. As with all school change efforts, this process of organizational change has not been as neat and seamless as it may appear from the above description, and the process of evaluation and improvement is ongoing. It has now been about a decade since the new program was implemented and the organizational changes within the Rossier School began. However, in terms of the cultural models and cultural settings discussed in the earlier part of this chapter, the before-and-after differences are notable and far-reaching. (See Marsh, Dembo, Gallagher, and Stowe (2010), for an account of this process and the rationale for change in more detail.)

It is notable that these changes have come about in a relatively short period, especially in a setting (not unlike that found in K–12 schools and districts) more known for long deliberation, resistance to change, and maintaining tradition. It seems that the Rossier School has successfully overcome many of the organizational gaps that were problematic prior to this shift, and has even managed to gain recognition for leadership in bringing about these changes (Shulman, Golde, Bueschel, & Garabedian, 2006).

Why is this example important for K–12 practitioners? There are a number of reasons. While the Rossier School of Education is a university setting and not a K–12 setting, the principles regarding how to address organizational gaps apply equally well. First, the example suggests that learning, motivation, and organizational issues can and do interact in complex ways. While this book treats them in separate chapters for convenience and clarity, all three need to be looked at as a dynamic and unified whole. If one were to address only single issues that characterized the school prior to the year 2000, for example, low faculty morale, or students' lack of knowledge about how to manage requirements to complete a degree, the impact would likely have been minimal, since so many organizational barriers to improved performance were involved. But the "big picture" lesson is that many times organizational issues are at the root of performance problems and can lead to additional motivational and learning gaps.

> Learning, motivation, and organizational issues interact in complex ways.

Second, the example should also be a good illustration of the fact that organizational change related to well-established cultural models and cultural settings is not easy—or quick. This change process took a decade and is still ongoing. Change had to be addressed at many different levels. Efforts to change educational organizations are better seen as a cyclical process that occur over time, rather than a linear process that is over in a short finite time span.

> Many times organizational issues are at the root of performance problems and can lead to additional motivational and learning gaps.

Third, when analyzing school-based performance problems, it is worth considering that there are sometimes good organizational reasons why people think or behave the way they do, even when it seems to be unproductive or worse. In this example, there were many. Before the changes noted above were implemented, there were many reasons behind low faculty morale and sometimes less than accommodating attitudes and behaviors toward students. For example, the school got very little recognition within the university except for negative reasons. There was frequent commentary about the relevance of the school and its programs. Many faculty members, like many K–12 teachers, felt like second-class citizens. In addition, the budget restrictions were a constant topic of discussion and threat, and often resulted in small or nonexistent raises, travel funds, supplies, and so forth. There was no common mission behind which faculty could marshal their efforts. This situation is all too familiar to leaders and teachers in public schools, where everyone from electioneering politicians to local business leaders, state department heads, and federal funders are all too willing to offer negative judgments.

In addition, during this time, as the University continued to develop as a major research university, the standards for tenure and promotion were becoming much more stringent. Many faculty members also felt overburdened by the competing demands to do research, publish, seek external funding, recruit new students, participate in seemingly endless rounds of committees and meetings, handle the day-to-day bureaucracy, and keep

> There are sometimes good organizational reasons why people think or behave the way they do, even when it seems to be unproductive or worse.

on top of paperwork requirements related to managing academic programs. One faculty member described the experience as mirroring the performance of a one-man band, where a single musician plays three, four, or five instruments within the same song. Doctoral students in my classes who work in urban school settings often express the same sentiment. Given the lack of sufficient infrastructure to help manage these competing demands, the calls to create a more student-friendly culture and environment tended to fall on deaf ears, and faculty sometimes acted in ways that at first glance would seem to be counterproductive. It is only by gaining an understanding of the ecological niche(s) within the school and the larger social context that the situation becomes a bit more understandable and amenable to change.

Finally, the approach matters. One approach to reform would have been to simply make structural changes by administrative fiat and then rain a set of mandates down on faculty and staff as is so commonly done in K–12 schools. There are many examples where this approach has been tried, including in a local school district where a specific highly structured reading program was mandated to boost student achievement, with rigid mechanisms built-in to assure teacher compliance. Not only were the results dubious, but teacher and student morale appeared to suffer in part because of the lack of autonomy and inability to meet individual needs. The most complaints seem to have come from the most experienced teachers, who were unable to use their skills and judgment, and instead had to follow the structured program.

One of the key factors in the change process at the Rossier School of Education was the collaboration that was enabled and became the norm. There was not a complete absence of administrative mandates, or complete agreement on the direction of the school, or specifics of the changes. Moreover, not every individual was able to include everything that he or she felt to be important. Indeed, the collaborative efforts were not and are not devoid of conflict. However, there was a degree of consensus about major decisions, and the perception of fairness and the perception of consideration of autonomy in decisionmaking were, for the most part, intact. Similar school reform and school change efforts in K–12 settings that attain some success and are sustained often share these important features (see Au [2009], for a good K–12 example).

ASSESSING AND EXAMINING CULTURAL MODELS AND SETTINGS

Previously it was noted that cultural models and settings may not be easy to measure, but they are amenable to being examined and described. If abstract concepts like cultural models or cultural settings are to be useful in considering educational performance problems, they should be observable and help understand why certain types of behaviors, policies, and practices make sense in a specific context. Therefore, when thinking about cultural models and settings for educational and related organizational settings, important questions include the following:

- What are the cultural models that characterize this organization? (beliefs, attitudes, ways of thinking and understanding, either implicit or explicit)
- What are the typical and characteristic activity settings in this organization? (normal as well as distinctive routines, formal and informal gatherings, meetings, and so on)
- What are typical activities within those settings? (What do people do in these settings and how do they behave?)
- How are they structured?
- How and when do they occur?
- Who participates?
- What are the spoken and unspoken rules? (What are the formal and informal policies, rules, regulations, norms, and other factors which suggest how people should or should not behave?)
- Who or what gets rewarded or sanctioned (either formally or informally)?
- How are decisions made?
- What are the circumstances that led to the current state of affairs?
- How do all of these dynamics promote or impede individual and organizational goals?

These questions provide important insights in to the organizational factors and dynamics that can have important influences on people's behavior. Once the cultural models and settings in a classroom, school, or even an entire district or educational organization are clear, it is easier to understand why people in that context think and behave and respond in the ways that they do. This understanding is the first step in changing these factors when they impede performance, or, alternatively, strengthening them when they enhance performance. While the school change and school reform literature provide useful ways of bringing about school change, it is absolutely essential that change not be done for its

> Once the cultural models and settings in a classroom, school, or even an entire district or educational organization are clear, it is easier to understand why people in that context think and behave and respond in the ways that they do.

> While the school change and school reform literature provide useful ways of bringing about school change, it is absolutely essential that change not be done for its own sake. Rather, change should be targeted at those specific features that impede goals.

own sake. Rather, the argument here is that change should be targeted at those specific features that impede organizational goals.

To summarize, the main questions of interest and importance in understanding educational settings, from classrooms to districts, are: What are the range of contexts in this organization or institution? What are the typical and common ones? Most importantly, do they facilitate or impede the achievement of goals? In attempting to answer these questions, it should be kept in mind that this process is not research in the traditional sense, but rather something more like focused inquiry. Some useful tools to collect information about these questions can be found in methods commonly used in qualitative inquiry, especially what is often called action research, participatory research, and related approaches (Ferrance, 2000; Mills, 2003; Noffke & Somekh, 2009). Examples of these tools include focus groups, interviews, observation, casual or more structured conversation, and so forth. These can be effectively applied in school settings to help develop an understanding of the prevailing culture and organizational structures and dynamics. There may be other situations where more quantitative approaches, such as structured surveys or inventories might be useful. However, the important thing is to get a valid, working understanding of the setting. There is evidence that even aspects of the organization, such as the quality and frequency of teacher-student interaction (Lundberg & Schreiner, 2004), or students' perceptions of things such as institutional barriers (Kenny, Blustein, Chaves, Grossman, & Gallagher, 2003) can be factors in successful student outcomes. It is important that these types of organizational gaps be systematically uncovered and considered along with knowledge and performance gaps in order to target solutions and expend resources in the most efficient manner possible.

CHAPTER 6

A Gap-Analysis Problem-Solving Approach

The previous three chapters have outlined the three critical areas of learning, motivation, and organizational factors that are important influences on whether the performance goals of a classroom, school, or district are met. When considered together, they can provide very useful information about why things may or may not be working well. However, in order to use the information, it is necessary to consider it in a systematic fashion before designing and evaluating possible solutions. What kinds of tools are available to schools and educational organizations to improve performance?

There are many problem-solving models in the educational literature that have been developed, in part spurred by increased accountability pressures (Elmore, 2003; see, for example, Boudett, City, & Murnane, 2007). Many publications focus on the use of data in educational decisionmaking to improve school performance (Holcomb, 1999; Johnson, 2002; Love, 2002; U.S. Department of Education, 2002), including studies that target specific aspects of learning and school improvement (e.g., Saunders, Goldenberg, & Gallimore, 2009). Some approaches based on comprehensive school reform models seek change in how educational organizations achieve their goals (see, for example, Datnow, Lasky, Stringfield, & Teddlie, 2006) while others tend to focus primarily on instructional issues (Brunner, et al., 2005; Halverson, Grigg, Pritchett, & Thomas, 2007).

This chapter presents the highlights of one such model, an approach called *gap analysis* (Clark & Estes, 2008. While this is a model that has its origins in the business world, it is highly applicable to problem-solving in educational settings (recognizing that K–12 schools are *not* business entities). It is used in the Urban School Leadership doctoral program at USC (see Marsh et al., 2010) as a way of incorporating a problem-solving orientation to the coursework of the working school professionals in the

Figure 6.1. An Overview of the Gap-Analysis Model

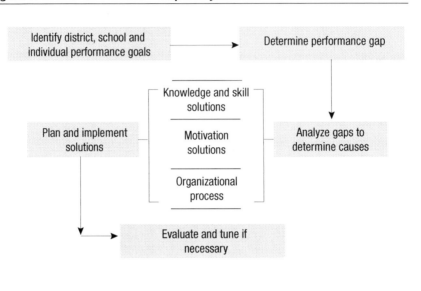

Source: Adapted from Clark, 2004, p. 21

program. In addition, the gap-analysis approach has been used to structure practice-based dissertation projects, giving doctoral students an opportunity to situate their studies in real school problems.

Why this model? As noted above, most organizational problem-solving approaches focus on organizational factors, while others focus on individual factors such as teacher, student, or administrator characteristics, but few, if any, focus on both. In addition, they tend to draw primarily from organizational theories of change, but typically don't draw heavily on learning and motivation theories *in addition* to organizational features, even when they consider instructional issues. In addition, while existing approaches are data driven, they often focus on the technology of data collection, or on creating a culture related to using data, or on data collection as a change strategy or on data as a decisionmaking tool. However, they do not always provide guidance on what exactly to collect on, or else they focus on one element, usually teaching and learning, but not others, like motivation, organization features, and so forth. (There are some exceptions, see Bernhardt, 2004.)

WHAT IS GAP ANALYSIS?

Gap analysis is a systematic problem-solving approach to improve performance and achieve organizational goals (Clark & Estes, 2008). It provides a way to clarify both short-term and long-term organizational and individual goals, assess them, and describe gaps from the actual levels of performance or achievement to the desired levels. It also provides a way to investigate and validate assumed causes of those gaps—rather than relying on guesswork—so that resources and solutions are clearly targeted to the most important causes of performance gaps. The gap-analysis process focuses on three areas that correspond to the information covered in Chapters 3, 4, and 5 (knowledge and skill, motivation, and organizational factors), and provides for the use of validated (i.e., research-based) solutions. Finally, it is designed to help real organizations improve their success by providing assistance in solving real-world problems, whether in a classroom, school, or district. It is suited to serve a range of educational organizations as a consultant model or as a model for organizations to use on their own. A general overview of the steps in the gap-analysis process is found in Figure 6.1.

WHAT ARE THE STEPS IN GAP ANALYSIS?

The general steps in the gap-analysis process are outlined in the following paragraphs (based on Clark & Estes, 2008).

Defining Goals

In the gap-analysis model, the first step consists of defining measurable goals at three levels: long-term (global goals), intermediate (or subsidiary goals leading to long-term goals), and day-to-day (performance) goals. (For those unfamiliar with goals, a good reference is Anderson & Krathwohl, 2001.) Goals answer the question, "What do we want to accomplish?" Goals are important for organizations in the same way they are for individuals, as the motivation literature would suggest. They not only provide direction, but they allow a

> Goals not only provide direction, but they allow a mechanism for determining when to change the present course of action.

mechanism for determining when to change the present course of action. Global goals typically take on the order of 1 to 5 years or more, intermediate goals typically take weeks to months, and performance or learning goals typically can be accomplished in days or hours.

For an entire educational organization or school, the long-term, or global goal, is often found in the mission statement. While most or all organizations have a mission statement, it is surprising how few are accompanied by measurable components or additional measurable goals. The mission statement provides a focusing general vision statement such as, "to assure that all students are successful" or "to produce educated students and productive citizens." These are laudable goals, and appropriate for a vision statement. Without then creating supporting measurable goals, how would one know whether the vision is informing practice and what progress remains to be made? The goal should not only be measurable but also provide enough information about the benchmark against which performance is being evaluated. For a school, as an example, an appropriate benchmark for student academic performance, graduation rates, attendance as a measure of engagement, reduction of discipline problems, and other common goals, might be similar schools in the district that are successful at achieving the goal in question. These benchmark entities can also be a source of information on how success has been achieved in other places.

Goals can be norm-based such as, "The goal is to have the lowest dropout rate in the district" (where performance is ranked against others), or criterion-based, "All graduating students will apply to at least one college" (where performance is ranked against a specific criterion).

Intermediate goals, at the next level down, specify what must be done in the shorter term in order to accomplish the global goal. It should be recognized that global goals, as the name implies, are wide-ranging and long term, and therefore can have many intermediate (and even more performance or short-term goals) that correspond to it. In general, goals at this level indicate what must be done in the short term in order to assure achievement of the global goal. These lower level goals are necessary because, just as with individuals, organizations can become discouraged and lose focus if they do not have current, concrete, and challenging goals. These help to

> Lower level goals are necessary because, just as with individuals, organizations can become discouraged and lose focus if they do not have current, concrete, and challenging goals. These help to *partialize* or decompose the larger task into manageable chunks.

partialize or decompose the larger task into manageable chunks. For example, if a global goal focuses on all high school seniors gaining acceptance by at least one college, intermediate goals might focus on making sure that all students understand the application process and paperwork, that student course loads beginning in the freshman year are monitored to ensure that they include courses that will be required for college entry, that all students are given instruction and practice in writing college essays, that students and parents receive counseling about necessary courses, tests, deadlines, and schedules, that programs are created to keep students from falling through the cracks when reading, writing, and math interventions will support their success, that special programs support needs of pregnant or otherwise challenged students (Casanova, 2010). While the global goal in this case might take several years, individual intermediate goals might be accomplished over the course of weeks to months.

Performance goals indicate what needs to be accomplished in the very short term. Following up on the last example, students would need to understand the different parts of a college application essay; how to distinguish an effective essay from an ineffective one; and know the difference between different types of colleges (e.g., 4-year versus community college), in order to tailor their own essay.

When considering goals, it is useful to think of a triangle or pyramid, where the global goal is at the top, and the myriad of other goals needed to achieve it are underneath. Some might focus on students, some might focus on teachers, and others might focus on administrators. It is useful to think here in terms of stakeholders. That is, what it is that each specific stakeholder in the context needs to achieve in order to achieve the global goal. In addition to considering all relevant stakeholders, attention should be paid to whether goals at all levels are measurable and that they are aligned, that is, that those at a lower level feed into the other levels. Goals should also have deadlines and specific criteria for knowing if they have been met.

Determining Gaps

Once goals have been determined, it is necessary to see how far from achieving them current performance is. This stage of the gap analysis answers the question, "How far are we from achieving our goals?" The focus at this

> Think of a triangle or pyramid, where the global goal is at the top, and the myriad of other goals needed to achieve it are underneath.

stage is to compare the goals to a standard that represents a desired level of performance or achievement. The gap is determined by subtracting current performance from the standard. For example, if our global goal was that all students who are seniors gain acceptance by at least one college, but only 45% currently do, then the gap here would be 55%. The same steps would be followed with the goals at the other levels. As another example, if a school's goal was to provide differentiated instruction, the percentage of teachers who can demonstrate competence in differentiating a lesson subtracted from 100% would represent the gap.

HYPOTHESIZING ABOUT POSSIBLE CAUSES

Causal analysis consists of listing and validating the possible causes that may be at the root of less than desired performance with respect to goals. The relevant question here is, "What are the most likely reasons that the gap(s) exist?" Specific attention is given to the areas of knowledge, motivation, and organizational/institutional factors as possible causes for the gap. This analysis should draw on the factors that have been discussed in the last three chapters. As specific causes are assessed and ruled out, a clearer picture can be obtained for what is likely causing the performance gap(s), and solutions can be targeted specifically at those areas. Unfortunately, this step is skipped in so many schools and organizations that have identified performance problems they want to address. Often, a cause is assumed and then acted on, or worse, an assumed cause leads to inaction because it seems insurmountable.

An example of assumed causes is found in a dissertation project[1] in which the dissertation group used a gap-analysis approach to investigate targeted performance issues in two school districts. In one of the two districts where the work took place, the teams of doctoral students focused on the depressed achievement of Latino students (specifically English Learners) within the district compared to other subgroups, and examined the low achievement of one high school relative to another high-performing high school in the same district. These issues were identified by the district as particular concerns.

> Often, a cause is assumed and then acted on, or worse, an assumed cause leads to inaction because it seems insurmountable.

It turns out that one of the assumed causes for low achievement by some teachers was that Latino students and their families were not interested in high achievement, did not see college as worthwhile, and were unmotivated to exert effort to achieve academic goals. For example, interviews with some teachers resulted in the following views: "Students do not feel it is important to learn English because they do not use it at home or even at school when they are with their friends," and "For the most part, the Hispanic parents do not really value their children learning English as long as they are in a school where the majority of the students look like them and there are no (social) problems." The problem is that these beliefs reflected *assumed* causes rather than *validated* causes, and no alternative explanations or possibilities were considered.

At the same time teachers were voicing these concerns, many complained of a lack of knowledge of the surrounding community and feeling inadequate in teaching students. As one teacher noted, "I don't know how to help them sometimes. I am not trained to teach these kids. So when they struggle I send them back to the ELD (English Language Development) teachers." Given these views, some staff felt that the causes for low achievement were not amenable to change based on their efforts and their motivation suffered. Because of these beliefs, interviews with teachers suggested that some or many teachers may have lowered their expectations and may have provided less challenging curricula to these students. There is a long history in the educational literature where similar circumstances can be found. While these assumed causes are common and may characterize a few students, there is ample literature to suggest that these perceptions may be misguided (Valencia, 2010). In fact, there is also some evidence that ideally, what teachers may assume to be cultural deficits and differences can in fact be used as valuable instructional resources (Gonzalez, Moll, & Amanti, 2005; Lee, 2007).

A similar example of jumping to conclusions regarding performance problems was noted in a meeting held as part of a university-based project (see Bensimon, Polkinghorne, Bauman, & Vallejo, 2004) on fostering equitable outcomes for diverse students in community college settings. The overall project was designed as an action project with several community college partners, organized as faculty and administrator teams from each institution, with the goal of facilitating inquiry into issues of equity on their own campuses. In addition to significant discrepancies in achievement across ethnic and racial groups, the success rate in the many remedial courses (heavily populated by diverse students) was notably lower at each of the participating campuses.

At one of the initial kick-off meetings, attendees were presented with information on ethnic and racial differences in achievement in community

> Making assumptions about causes for performance problems only becomes a problem when those assumptions are treated as fact in the absence of any validation, and when alternative possibilities are ignored. Acting on assumed causes when they are in fact incorrect only compounds the problem.

college settings. Small groups were then formed to participate in an exercise that asked them to generate as many possible causes for the achievement differences as they could. At the end of the exercise, the lists that were generated by each group were collected and later examined. A striking similarity across groups was that almost every cause that was listed by the groups was focused on student deficits—low motivation, poor preparation, effects of poverty, and so on. Almost no attention was paid to external factors such as poor instruction, onerous requirements to get through remedial courses, lack of tutoring and counseling resources, and so forth. A look at the campuses suggested that many of the existing projects and activities aimed at remedying the achievement issues built on these assumed causes—but none were designed to look at the issue of instruction and improving faculty competence to deal with a changing population. Unfortunately, this is not an isolated example, since this pattern has been found repeatedly at different times and in many other settings during the course of the project.

What is wrong with speculating about the causes of low performance in school settings? Absolutely nothing. In fact, it is an important part of the gap-analysis process. Moreover, there is a whole area of work in motivation that focuses on the attributions people make about the causes for success and failure on various activities or tasks. Making assumptions about causes for performance problems only becomes a problem when those assumptions are treated as fact in the absence of any validation, and when alternative possibilities are ignored. Acting on assumed causes when they are in fact incorrect only compounds the problem.

> An alternative to making assumptions about causes is to list them and investigate them directly so that the nature of the problem is understood, and the solutions are directly targeted to the actual roots of the problem.

A common reaction to performance problems in many schools I have visited is to assume that teachers lack knowledge and need more professional development. Often, other possibilities are not considered. Nevertheless, as the previous chapters have tried to convey, there are often other or additional reasons. An alternative to making assumptions about causes is to list them and investigate them directly so that the nature of the problem is understood, and the solutions are directly targeted to the actual roots of the problem. The general idea is to focus on the areas of knowledge and skill, motivation, and organization culture and structure, and look at how each of these may or may not be contributing to the problem and how each can contribute to the solution.

Validating and Prioritizing Causes

There are many ways to investigate whether hypothesized causes are in fact really problems, some of which were mentioned in the last chapter. Interviews, focus groups, observations, surveys, informal conversations, among others, are useful tools, although more structured surveys and interviews can at times be helpful. What is most useful in any given setting is determined by a variety of factors, such as the size of the school or district, the number of people involved, the willingness, and comfort level of people to be candid, and so on. While the gap-analysis approach is not research in the traditional sense, and the data collection methods are not judged by the same scientific standards, reliability and validity of the information gathered is critical. Specifically, is your understanding of the situation accurate? If another person were to examine the same setting, would he or she come to the same conclusions that you did? Various methodologies that can be useful in gap analysis are used in traditional research activities, and can be adapted for the gap analysis's purposes. A useful rule of thumb that is often used in qualitative research studies is that one check on the accuracy of your understanding of a setting is that the people in that setting would agree that you have captured the essence of that setting. It is best to think of this stage of the gap analysis as detective work that helps narrow down the list of assumed causes and helps develop a more accurate understanding of the root causes of performance problems.

It will usually be the case that there will be several, rather than one, cause or gap that is leading to not achieving goals. After all, schools are complex social settings. In this case, it is best to prioritize the list of causes according to both cost (in terms of time and resources and difficulty of implementation) and to how central the gap is to causing the problem being addressed. Which cause, if it were

> It will usually be the case that there will be several, rather than one, cause or gap that is leading to not achieving goals.

> If too many things are addressed at the same time, it is likely that goals will become diffuse, the task will seem overwhelming, and resources may become strained.

addressed, would lead to the greatest possibility of achieving the goals? Since it is probable that not everything can be solved at the same time, it is a good idea to step back and consider the trade-offs of one course of action versus other alternatives. If too many things are addressed at the same time, it is likely that goals will become diffuse, the task will seem overwhelming, and resources may become strained.

Developing Solutions

One key to solutions being effective is that they are targeted at the causes. In the gap- analysis framework, the major categories of causes emphasized, as we have seen, are in the domains of learning (knowledge and skills), motivation, and organizational factors. This step of the gap analysis answers the question, "What can we do to fix it?"

Where does one turn after specific causes have been narrowed down? It is good to stop and consider what type of cause is being targeted. As we have seen from the previous chapters, the three most likely areas where gaps are found are in the areas of knowledge, motivation, and organizational factors. Thus, it is good to group causes accordingly, since addressing each type of cause requires a different approach. Having said that, however, it is important to keep in mind that in the real world, these areas are intertwined in complex ways. Nevertheless, as a starting point, it is good to consider these categories independently, and make sure to match solutions to the specific type of cause being targeted.

As an example, consider the problem of aggressive behavior among students. In some schools, it is a critical factor that impedes the ability to achieve important academic goals. Let us consider for a moment some possible causes. It is possible that students act aggressively because they attribute minor social transgressions, such as an accidental bump in a school hallway, as an aggressive social challenge. They may perceive aggression as the easiest or only avenue for increasing their social status within the school. They may lack knowledge about appropriate social responses for keeping such minor social conflicts from escalating into encounters that

> Consider the problem of aggressive behavior among students. In some schools, it is a critical factor that impedes the ability to achieve important academic goals.

are more aggressive. There may be an attitude of tolerance at the school for such aggression, lack of appropriate supervision of students, inconsistent or lax enforcement of school discipline, or lack of meaningful consequences for offenders. Let us assume that all of these causes have in fact been found to be true in the school. In order to eliminate the problem, all of these causes would likely need to be addressed. In considering solutions, however, it would be key to match them with the type of issue being addressed. For example, organizational changes like improving the supervision and enforcement policies regarding aggression will not address the motivational beliefs of students about the assumed aggressive intentions of their peers. Nor will it address the knowledge gap about ways to respond appropriately to minor social transgressions. A comprehensive solution would need to address all of the assumed causes, but would need to assure that the solution is matched to the cause being targeted.

Where does one begin to find solutions to knowledge, motivation, and organizational gaps that are leading to performance problems? A good place to start is to consult the available research. Does this mean that an exhaustive, dissertation-like literature review needs to be completed before looking for solutions? It does not. It does mean that it is useful to scan existing work on the specific area that is being targeted for ideas about solutions.

The web is the easiest way to access research, and sources such as Google Scholar are enormously useful. Using the example of aggressive school behavior, a search with the keywords *aggressive school behavior* retrieves a number of relevant and informative sources. However, a word of caution is in order, since not all things found on the web are equally useful. The most credible sources are those that have undergone peer review. Reputable academic journals, for example, subject published articles to blind peer review by established scholars in the field. This assures adherence to basic standards of quality review and credibility. Some sources found on the web can be unscholarly, inaccurate, or biased. Nevertheless, there are a growing number of legitimate research guides, full-text collections, and other scholarly tools on the web worth exploring. Educational organizations and nonprofit websites are often good resources at the beginning stages of research. Rules of thumb are: Consider the source of the information, recognize that more recent sources are in general preferable to dated sources, and keep in mind that sources that have undergone some type of review process are preferable to those that have not. In general, the least preferable sources are those that are mainly the opinion of the author (no matter how famous), that have some kind of commercial connection, that come from popular sources (e.g., magazines, newspapers, newsletters) as opposed to academic sources (such as academic journals), or that are available from a source that is known as an advocate for a particular point of view. Reviews of research are especially valuable, if they exist, since they summarize, synthesize, and evaluate the available evidence on a given topic.

In the example of school aggression mentioned above, one study that would be found in a search was conducted by Hudley, Graham, and Taylor (2007). The study describes an intervention program that was implemented in a public-school setting around the issue of school aggression. The program provides details about the intervention, which targeted the motivational beliefs and social behaviors of students to help reduce peer violence and aggression. In addition to providing the details of the intervention, the article provided empirical evidence about the positive effects the program had on reducing the problem. This article could provide a very useful resource in thinking about how a school might tackle a similar problem as that described by Hudley and her colleagues.

It is a fact of life that there will be more research on some problems than on others, and, as is the case with many educational issues, sometimes there are no definitive answers. Education, after all, is not equivalent to medicine, where often problems and solutions are more unambiguously and closely linked. While there is a strong emphasis on research-based solutions in the gap-analysis approach, it is also true that there is not complete agreement in the academic community about the meaning of terms like *research-based* and *scientific research* (Eisenhart & Towne, 2003; National Research Council, 2002). The most direct attempt to promote an evidence-based approach to educational interventions is found in the federal What Works Clearinghouse that provides reviews of the scientific merits of specific educational interventions (see http://ies.ed.gov/ncee/wwc/). While the Clearinghouse has been sharply criticized for both the narrowness of the criteria used to evaluate studies, with its emphasis on randomized clinical trials and scientific neutrality (see, for example, Berliner, 2002; Schoenfeld, 2006), it can be a useful resource. It should not replace an independent search of the available literature, which can provide useful information where no other guidance exists.

An additional source for possible solutions for specific types of problems can be found in various theoretical approaches to learning and motivation. Table 6.1, for example, provides an example of some of the specific theoretical perspectives and the various tools they offer that could be of potential use in designing solutions to specific performance gaps, especially those involving knowledge and motivation gaps. While this table is overly simplistic, and the admittedly imprecise use of labels is certain to raise eyebrows in some quarters, the purpose here is not to stress comprehensiveness or fidelity to detailed distinctions among approaches. Rather, the goal is to illustrate how some of the tools can be appropriated to deal with specific validated causes.

Table 6.1. Educational Interventions and Remediation Perspectives from Various Learning Theories

Approach	Focus	Examples in Practice
Behavioral	Focus on external behavior, change external environment	Incentive systems, applied behavior analysis interventions, rearrange contingencies in social environment
Cognitive	Individual learning strategies and cognitive processes	Cognitive, mnemonic, and metacognitive strategy training
Social Cognitive	Learning related beliefs and values that impact active choice, persistence, and effort; vicarious learning and modeling	Motivation-related interventions (attributions, self-efficacy, task value, etc.); modeling; self-regulation
Social Constructivist	The social and cultural nature of teaching and learning; role of cultural tools and mediation in learning	Scaffolding, peer instruction; collaborative learning, funds of knowledge, connections to real-world activities, cultural accommodation (social organization of classroom, discourse features, content, and materials), multicultural education
Organizational	Organizational structure, practices, and policies	School reform and restructuring
Critical theory, sociopolitical approaches	Intergroup power relations, political and social issues as manifested in local settings	Critical instructional practices, empowerment strategies as an essential part of education

> Existing programs in other schools or districts can be a useful source of information in finding solutions, but there should be some evidence that it actually does make a difference. There are many reasons why a specific problem may get better or worse, and without some evidence, it should not be assumed that a specific program or initiative was the cause.

Existing programs in other schools or districts can be a useful source of information in finding solutions, but there should be some evidence that it actually does make a difference. There are many reasons why a specific problem may get better or worse, and without some evidence, it should not be assumed that a specific program or initiative was the cause. Whichever sources are drawn upon in devising solutions, however, it is important that they be evaluated regarding appropriateness for the local situation. Interventions may have been successful in contexts that may be very different from the conditions in a given school or district, and automatic replication of the same results should not be assumed. In addition, proposed solutions to knowledge, motivation, and organizational gaps should be examined along with other critical dimensions relevant to the local ecology such as the following (Plato Learning, 2003, p. 2):

- Affordability (Where will we get the money?)
- Adoptability (Can we use it?)
- Acceptability (Will people agree to use it?)
- Substitutability (What will this replace in order to free needed energy and other resources to support?)

Figure 6.2 and Table 6.2 provide a brief example of what a targeted gap analysis might entail. Note that this is only an example. In the real world, it is possible that many more intermediate and performance goals might be added in order to capture the complexity of the problem and the context. However, it does provide a view for what might be entailed in addressing the issue of school aggression from this perspective.

The final chapter provides additional considerations related to cultural and contextual factors that can inform decisions at this stage of the process. The main point here is that the available research is always preferable to intuition, which can often be wrong, or tradition ("this is how we have always done it"), which can perpetuate ineffective approaches.

> Research is always preferable to intuition, which can often be wrong, or tradition ("this is how we have always done it"), which can perpetuate ineffective approaches.

Figure 6.2. An Example of the Elements of a Gap Analysis: Goals, Measures, Standards, and Gaps for a Middle School Trying to Reduce Aggression-Related Conflicts

Global Goal: Mission School will provide a safe school environment for all students

Measure: Number of discipline-related events reported

Standard: First year standard = match school in the district with the lowest number of incidents; Five year standard = zero incidents reported

Gap: 120 incidents reported during the last school year

Intermediate Goal: All students will be able to respond in a socially appropriate way to minor social transgressions by peers

Measure: Number and distribution of aggression-related conflicts by student

Standard: No aggression-related conflicts for any student

Gap: 50 students were involved in conflicts during the last year, 25 of these students were involved in more than one conflict

Performance Goal 1: When provided an example of a minor social transgression, students will be able to describe appropriate versus inappropriate attributions

Measure: Paper/pencil scenario

Standard: 100%

Gap: 80% of the student body met the standard, but only 10% of those involved in conflicts met the standard

Performance Goal 2: When provided an example of a minor social transgression, students will be able to describe appropriate social strategies to de-escalate the potential conflict

Measure: Paper/pencil scenario

Standard: 100%

Gap: 75% of the student body met the standard, but only 12% of those involved in conflicts met the standard

---

Interventions may have been successful in contexts that may be very different from the conditions in a given school or district, and automatic replication of the same results should not be assumed. Proposed solutions to knowledge, motivation, and organizational gaps should be examined along other critical dimensions relevant to the local ecology.

Table 6.2. An Example of the Elements of a Gap Analysis: Causes, Measures, and Solutions

		Assessed by:	Validated?	Solution	Evaluation
Possible Causes: Knowledge	Students do not have conflict resolution strategies	Scenario	Yes	Conflict resolution skills intervention program modeled after Hudley et al., (2007)	Increased knowledge about strategies
	Students do not realize the consequences of aggressive behavior	Interviews	Yes		Recognition of consequences of aggression
	Students cannot discriminate minor transgressions from actual threats	Scenario	Yes		Ability to discriminate imagined vs. real threats
Possible Causes: Motivation	Students see no consequences for aggressive behavior		Yes	Attribution retraining intervention modeled after Hudley (2007) but also including information on the causes and consequences of violence	Students recognize consequences
	Aggression is seen as an easy way to gain social status		Yes		Students can specify alternative ways to gain status
	Students make incorrect attributions about minor social transgressions		Yes		Students are able to make appropriate attributions
Possible Causes: Organizational	Inconsistent consequences		Yes	Examine and revise discipline policies; shift resources to provide supervision in "high incidence" location of the school; assign responsibility to monitor conflicts to one person	Consistent policy with specified consequences adopted
	Lax consequences		Yes		
	Lack of supervision		Yes		Resources shifted
	Tolerance of incidents to avoid negative fallout		Yes		Consistent monitoring of response monitored and reported; sanctions possible

EVALUATING OUTCOMES

The final step in the gap-analysis process is to evaluate the outcomes. It is important to keep in mind that just because so-lutions seem like they *should* work does not mean they *will* work. Therefore, this stage of the gap-anal-ysis process answers the question, "Did it work?" It is important to examine the results of solutions to make sure they actually solve the performance

> Just because solutions seem like they *should* work does not mean they *will* work.

problems they were intended to address or that they have not led to other unintended consequences.

Although evaluation can be a complex, costly, and politically sensitive undertaking, it does not have to be. Our doctoral courses in urban leader-ship in which we teach leaders to use this model are comprised primarily of educational practitioners without extensive backgrounds in evaluation. For the most part, we have relied on the relatively straightforward work of Clark and Estes (2008), who drew on the earlier work of Kirkpatrick (2006), and Kirkpatrick and Kirkpatrick (2006) because of their evaluation model's simplicity and utility for school settings. While it was originally developed with a focus on evaluating training and could be used to mea-sure the success of professional development and the progress of profes-sional learning communities toward identified goals, it is generalizable enough to be used in a variety of settings and for a variety of purposes. Basically, the model outlines four levels of evaluation:

- *Level 1: Reaction*—What do people feel or think about the solution?
- *Level 2: Impact*—Did the solution result in changes in the learning (knowledge and skill), motivation, and organizational gaps identi-fied earlier?
- *Level 3: Transfer*—Did the solution continue to be implemented and be effective after the solution was introduced?
- *Level 4: Bottom Line Results*—Did the solution contribute to meet-ing the overall global goal?

> It is important to examine the results of solutions to make sure they actually solve the performance problems they were intended to address or that they have not led to other unintended consequences.

Level 1 is essentially a measure of motivation. It assesses how satisfied or how enthusiastic people are about implementing one or more solutions to performance gaps. As we have seen earlier, motivation is not trivial, because it impacts whether people choose to engage in an activity, whether they persist, and whether they exert sufficient effort. Often this is assessed using feedback forms, surveys, and questionnaires; but it can also be assessed more informally by some of the other methods mentioned previously, such as interviews, focus groups, and so on. It is important to note that sometimes *any* innovation will result in initial enthusiasm, which can quickly wane. Alternatively, sometimes people will express negative reactions to *any* new innovation, for example because they have negative feelings toward the person or group who developed it, because it challenges the accepted way of doing things, or because it changes power relationships or work responsibilities. There is a diminished chance that a solution introduced to help close a performance gap will be effective if there are problems at Level I.

Level 2 focuses on whether there have been changes in the knowledge and skill, motivational, and organizational areas that were targeted as root causes for the performance gaps uncovered. The most effective ways of looking at this level involve direct assessment as opposed to self-report assessments. If the solution was targeting a knowledge or skill gap, asking a person whether they have mastered a skill or procedure of some area of critical knowledge can provide some information, but assessments that look at this more directly are more informative. In addition, the information on the Anderson & Krathwohl (2001) taxonomy covered in Chapter 3 should remind us that there are different ways that you can know something. *Remembering* something is different, for example, than being able to *apply, analyze, evaluate,* or *create* something with the knowledge that one has acquired. If the knowledge gap involves areas other than learning, it is also more desirable to observe changes in these areas directly. If the

> Motivation is not trivial, because it impacts whether people choose to engage in an activity, whether they persist, and whether they exert sufficient effort.

> Sometimes *any* innovation will result in initial enthusiasm. Sometimes people will express negative reactions to *any* new innovation, because they have negative feelings toward the person or group who developed it, because it challenges the accepted way of doing things, or because it changes power relationships or work responsibilities.

solution was designed to target an organizational gap, then evidence for that change should be sought.

Level 3 focuses on transfer. There are a couple of ways to consider transfer, for example transfer across time, across contexts, or even across tasks. The most basic concern at this level, however, is whether the solution is implemented in the relevant contexts and whether it is sustained over time, past the initial introduction. If the solution involved training, can people apply what they learned in a real-world context? Moreover, do they continue to apply what they learned over time? As with the other levels, there are a variety of methods to track this, but the more direct the assessment the better. Self-report can be a useful source of information, but it should not be the only one.

Level 4 focuses on the overall purpose for engaging in the gap-analysis process in the first place. Evaluation at this level answers the question whether the global goal is being or has been closed. This is one reason why it is critical that the goals be measurable. If the solutions fail to impact the overall goals, then they are the wrong solutions, or alternatively the right solutions to the wrong problem. It would be unrealistic, especially given complex global goals with a variety of cascading goals and a range of validated causes in all three areas, to expect rapid change. Although there is no hard and fast rule for what constitutes a reasonable time span, and this needs to be determined depending on the local ecology. If the target of the solution is a long-standing and well-entrenched belief, attitude, or practice, impacting the goal may take more time than other targets, which might show progress more rapidly.

> If the target of the solution is a long-standing and well-entrenched belief, attitude, or practice, impacting the goal it may take more time.

In sum, gap analysis is a systematic problem-solving method to help diagnose and solve organizational problems. It is a way of engaging in problem-solving while focusing on the most common reasons for performance gaps. It is important to recognize that the gap-analysis process has been presented as a linear problem-solving model, but it should be more accurately seen as a cyclical model. It helps by clarifying goals, assessing current performance, and targeting solutions and resources most effectively at areas that are most central to the problems identified. It provides a systematic way to examine the results of efforts to address performance gaps. In Chapter 7, the focus is on special considerations related to cultural and contextual factors that characterize educational organizations and institutions. These factors form the complex sociocultural contexts that make up the daily lives of schools, where problems and solutions unfold; and they are important considerations.

Taking Social, Cultural, and Contextual Processes into Account

The previous chapters have outlined a systematic process for thinking about both organizational and school goals at different levels as well as for identifying specific factors that might be impeding the achievement of those goals. This problem-solving approach focused specifically on identifying gaps related to knowledge, motivation, and organizational issues; on validating causes for those gaps; and developing and evaluating solutions to target the specific causes for those identified gaps. It is easy to think about the previous chapters in a mechanistic way, where the process is followed in a lock-step fashion without considering the complexities and interrelationships in the social context being examined.

It is important to keep in mind, however, that places like schools are comprised of individuals who interact in complex ways with each other and who create the social contexts they inhabit. Unless this point is kept in mind, change efforts can lead to the adoption of piecemeal solutions and attempts to scale up solutions that ignore important cultural and contextual dynamics. While implementing solutions to specific problems and trying to scale up change, it is critical to remember that something that works in one place may not work in another, or may work for entirely different reasons. A good example is found in the area of special education as presented below.

> Schools are comprised of individuals who interact in complex ways with each other and who create the social contexts they inhabit.

THE CASE OF SPECIAL EDUCATION AND OVERREPRESENTATION

As an example of the importance of the points just mentioned, consider the case of the assessment and referral process of special education.

Almost 4 decades ago researchers such as Mercer (1973) uncovered significant disparities based on race and ethnicity in the numbers of students placed in certain categories of special education. At the time, the biggest problem was the placement of African American and Latino students in the category of mild mental retardation. While the fact that there were exceptionally large numbers of these students

> Something that works in one place may not work in another, or may work for entirely different reasons.

in special education was not debated, the causes were hotly contested, and decades of debate and controversy ensued. The presumed causes ranged from genetically related cognitive deficiencies, to discriminatory assessment measures and procedures, to institutional racism, to lack of opportunity to learn, among other factors (Waitoller, Artiles, & Cheney, 2010). The controversy and concern about this problem resulted in a major report by the National Research Council (Heller, Holtzman, & Messick, 1982). In spite of this report, however, the problem and controversy persisted, and a second national study and report were completed on the same topic (National Research Council, 2002).

While the problem of overrepresentation in special education has not disappeared (Artiles, Rueda, Salazar, & Higareda, 2002; Harry & Klinger, 2006; Harry, Klinger, & Cramer, 2007), it has decreased, and the attention has resulted in some changes in the referral and assessment process. For example, the traditional approach to special education placement required a student to first exhibit significant educational difficulties before a referral for testing could be made by a teacher, and before relevant services could be provided within the special education system. This was true even if teachers suspected a problem much earlier and wanted to be proactive in addressing minor learning problems that could become more severe if left unaddressed. A common criticism of the traditional referral and assessment process was that IQ tests and similar assessments did not give teachers much information on which to base instruction, but merely confirmed the existence of a problem that they had already suspected existed. When the costs of doing psychometric assessments and other problems related to the traditional assessment and referral process were considered, many in the field began looking for alternatives. Thus, one of the recommendations of the 2002 National Research Council report was to move away from a test-based IQ assessment process for special education referral and placement purposes. That is, rather than relying on standardized IQ score cutoffs to determine eligibility, the report suggested a more educational approach that focused on response to intervention. The intent of this new approach was to allow for earlier, more proactive, and more education-ally relevant intervention that would help rule out instructional problems stemming from student learning difficulties.

In December 2004, Congress passed the Individuals with Disabilities Education Improvement Act (IDEIA, 2004), which permitted local educa-tion agencies to use a Response-to-Intervention (RTI) approach for iden-tifying children with possible learning disabilities for special education. With the passage of IDEIA, educators were essentially given the choice of using the traditional IQ achievement discrepancy model or RTI pro-cedures for identifying students at-risk for a Specific Learning Disability (SLD), one of the categories that has historically been problematic with respect to the overrepresentation problem.

The basis of RTI is to provide educational intervention at increasing levels of intensity and then carefully documenting how an individual responds. Rather than making inferences about an individual's learning characteristics based on tests, RTI permits an assessment of how they ac-tually do respond to increasingly intense levels of intervention (Fuchs, Mock, Morgan, & Young, 2003). RTI is meant to be implemented in the general education setting. It is only at the more intensive levels that spe-cial education is considered as a possibility. If a student responds to RTI procedures, then a referral to special education is averted. A central part of the RTI model is that the instructional practices or interventions at each of the successively more intense levels should be based on scientific evidence about what works.

In theory, the overall model holds a great deal of promise for dealing with a major organizational issue that has long plagued special education practitioners and those they serve. Yet, the field has been slow to make a change. While the model has worked as intended in some places, many districts and schools struggle to make sense of and implement the newer approach. In some of these places, the training and expertise needed to successfully implement the RTI approach does not exist or is minimal. In other schools, where the demographics of the community and school have rapidly changed and become more diverse, some practitioners have found it difficult to implement the RTI model. For example, some have questioned whether there are sufficient documented and well-researched interventions that have been designed for specific groups, such as English Learners. Without an array of well-researched interventions, the foun-dation of the model is open to question. The universality of educational interventions is open to past as well as current debate (Au & Mason, 1983; Goldenberg, 2008). However, Klinger & Edwards (2006) raise exactly this issue with respect to RTI:

> It is essential to find out what works with whom, by whom, and in what contexts. We ask, what should the first tier look like for culturally diverse students? For English-language learners? For students living in high-poverty areas? What should the second tier look like? Should it be the same for all? If not, how should it vary, and how should this be determined? How can we make sure that the instruction is in fact responsive to children's needs? (p. 108)

Thus while the promise of RTI is great, there are cultural and contextual factors that have been important in determining how successfully the approach has been in specific settings. While the account of the complex issues related to special education overrepresentation presented above is overly simplified, the purpose is to reiterate the point that the ideas in Chapters 1–6 need to be considered with respect to the cultural and contextual factors within specific settings or sociocultural contexts.

Similar points could be made with respect to a completely different area, specifically language programs for English Learners. While the field of language instruction for students who are in the process of acquiring English is no less impacted by controversy than special education, there is a parallel that also highlights the role of social context in the area of language programs for students learning English.

> While the promise of RTI is great, there are cultural and contextual factors which have been important in determining how successfully the approach has been in specific settings.

PROGRAMS FOR ENGLISH LEARNERS

Second language immersion programs were originally developed in Canada in the 1960s and 1970s for English-speaking parents who were concerned about their children becoming proficient bilinguals in English and French. Language immersion is a method of language instruction in which the school curriculum is taught through the second language. At the time the programs were developed and implemented, the goal of attaining complete bilingualism for students was a strong value in the country, and proponents envisioned strong support for both languages. Students in these programs were fluent in their native language (English), and the programs were conceived as additive in the sense of providing a positive educational enrichment experience. These programs have a strong track record and have been successfully implemented in the Canadian context (Johnson & Swain, 1997; Swain, 2000) (although, as Swain, 2000, suggests, more recently changing political conditions may be eroding support for this approach).

In contrast to the Canadian situation, the U.S. context has been much different (Garcia, 2005). While there are language programs that are additive in nature and promote bilingual skills (Genesee & Lindholm-Leary, 2007), in some places language education has been much more contentious (Crawford, 2004), with a strong sentiment toward proficiency in English (Genesee, Lindholm-Leary, Saunders, & Christian, 2006). For example, in 1998, California voters overwhelmingly approved Proposition 227, an initiative that largely eliminated bilingual education in the state's public schools. Under the California initiative, most English Learners in that state are now placed in English-immersion programs. Arizona voters followed suit by passing Proposition 203, a proposal similar to the California initiative, in 2000. In both California and Arizona, the proportion of English Learners in bilingual education classes decreased from about one third to 11% after the initiatives became law. In 2002, Massachusetts's voters approved the ballot initiative in their state, doing away with the oldest bilingual education law in the nation (although Colorado voters rejected a similar initiative in their state).

Also in contrast to the Canadian situation, the largest target population for language education in the United States is comprised of students who are poor, immigrants, or children of immigrants, Spanish-speaking, with minimal schooling in their native language. While immersion programs can take a variety of forms, and may include the goal of proficiency in two languages (Cummins, 1998; Genesee, 1985), the English immersion programs for these students have tended to be seen as remedial rather than additive (Valenzuela, 1999), with no concern for maintenance of the native language. While the Canadian model appeared promising to many as a useful option in the United States, under these conditions the results have been much more mixed (August & Shanahan, 2006; Genesee, Lindholm-Leary, & Saunders, 2005). Hopes of transporting the relatively successful Canadian model to the very different sociocultural context of the United States in order to achieve the same results did not materialize. This example again serves to highlight the importance of the social and cultural context in thinking about solutions to performance problems. In the next section, this issue is addressed directly.

THE NATURE OF SCHOOL PERFORMANCE PROBLEMS

As Chapter 1 noted, in spite of many noteworthy attempts to remedy disparities in student performance, success has been modest except in isolated settings or on narrowly derived outcomes. It was argued that three important reasons were 1. the *fragmentation* of approaches, 2. the *misalignment* of approaches and goals, and 3. the *failure to match solutions* to problems. The issues of misalignment and of matching solutions to problems are best addressed in the problem-solving approach outlined in Chapter 6. By examining and aligning goals at different levels of the organizational system, and by drawing on research (not narrowly defined) and theory, these problems can be meaningfully approached. Here, we focus on the issue of fragmentation.

The Unit of Analysis Issue

In some ways, the issue of fragmentation can be seen as a *unit of analysis* issue—that is, what is the appropriate target to address? In efforts to deal with performance problems in schools, fragmentation is in part a function of how the relevant knowledge and theories are organized—that is, by specific disciplines. These disciplinary lines are evident in places like universities and in the journals and publications that are used to disseminate new knowledge in the field. It is very hard to break these virtual chains that serve to filter how problems and solutions are conceived and addressed. As Table 3.2 illustrated, learning theorists tend to focus on internal cognitive processes and the features of the cognitive system; motivation theorists tend to focus on the beliefs individuals have about things like specific tasks and their ability to succeed; sociocultural theorists tend to focus on features of context and cultural processes; critical theorists tend to focus on the power relationships and sociopolitical issues among groups; economically oriented theorists tend to focus on financial budgetary, financial, and resource-allocation issues; and organizational theorists focus on the structures and processes of organizations and institutions and how they can influence performance. Which of these is the right perspective?

At one level, they are all right. They all provide useful lenses to examine performance problems, and provide useful tools to help solve them. However, it is worth recalling the old adage that if the only tool one has is a hammer, then everything looks like a nail. Fixing the flat tire on a car but not the broken carburetor, because one only knows how to fix tires, will not

> Fixing the flat tire on a car but not the broken carburetor, because one only knows how to fix tires, will not help the car get back on the road.

Figure 7.1. Contextual Factors Influencing Student Achievement

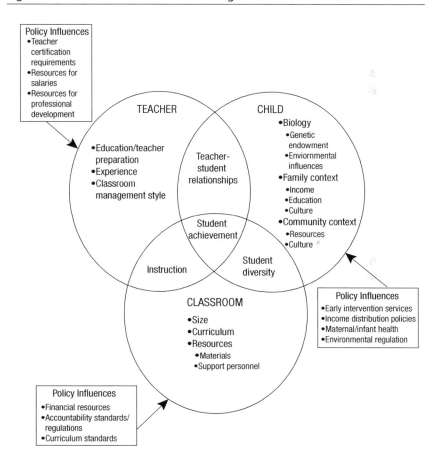

Note: This figure illustrates the myriad of factors that need to be considered in addressing student achievement issues. *Source*: Adapted from Donovan & Cross, 2002, p. 29

help the car get back on the road. Does that mean that knowing how to fix a flat tire is bad, or that fixing it was the wrong thing to do? Obviously not—it just was not the *only* thing to do to get the car running. If one's theory of automobiles extends only to tires, it is not likely that the car will be on the road for long. Yet, often complex performance problems in schools are approached the same way.

The Importance of the Local Ecology in Adopting Solutions

Many schools, especially in urban school settings, have significant issues with student reading and literacy achievement, for example. A common approach is to adopt a packaged instructional intervention that has been shown to work based on research findings where it was originally developed, or on findings where it was tried in other places. However, rarely is the question asked, how is that setting alike or different than *this* setting? In addition, how will the solution contribute to fixing the overall problem? A research-based phonics, or decoding, or vocabulary program may address important aspects of reading for students who are behind in reading. It may even help raise scores on measures designed to tar-

> Recall the overall goal—facilitating the development of students who have acquired expertise, are engaged, can self-regulate, and who achieve on a wide variety of outcomes in and out of school.

get growth in these areas. But if students are not encouraged to leverage the skills they have acquired toward understanding, not just decoding, text, or toward engaging with complex academic tasks, the overall long-term benefits may be minimal. This may also be exacerbated if students have little access to print materials at home, few library facilities in the community, teachers with low expectations, and problems related to poverty, such as poor living conditions. Recall the discussion in Chapter 1 (Figure 1.2) and the overall goal—facilitating the development of students who have acquired expertise, are engaged, can self-regulate, and who achieve on a wide variety of outcomes in and out of school.

Sociocultural Influences in Students' Learning

Many school performance problems focus on the learning problems of individual students or groups of students. Considering social and cultural processes is equally important in this area. Cognitive development, from

Figure 7.2. Multiple, Interacting Planes of Development. Rogoff's (2003) Conceptualization of the Unit of Analysis for Learning and Development

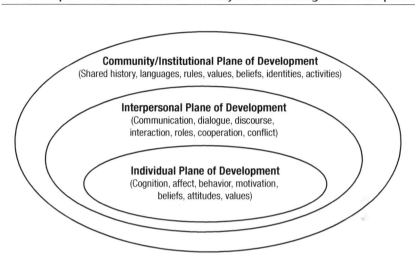

Community/Institutional Plane of Development
(Shared history, languages, rules, values, beliefs, identities, activities)

Interpersonal Plane of Development
(Communication, dialogue, discourse, interaction, roles, cooperation, conflict)

Individual Plane of Development
(Cognition, affect, behavior, motivation, beliefs, attitudes, values)

Source: Adapted from Rogoff, 2003

a sociohistorical perspective, involves the internalization of skills and other learned behaviors from participation in joint problem-solving activity with more competent others (adults, peers, etc.). Cole (1985) suggests that it is within this zone that culture and cognition create each other, where the cultural tools from past generations are acquired, practiced, and, in the process, transformed for later generations. A key assumption for this theory is that cultural, historical, and institutional factors reflect and shape an individual's mental processes, and language is an important mediator between learning and development. This view of cultural historical approach focuses on individuals' and groups' histories of participation in cultural practices and their experience in cultural activities, and provides a useful understanding of students' diverse learning process.

Drawing on this framework, Rogoff (1995, 2003) and Gutierrez & Rogoff (2003) provide a useful set of questions that might guide practitioners in investigating these learning-related cultural practices of students. These include the following: What is the range and nature of settings that the learner has had experience with? Who are/were the participants? What is the range and nature of things people do/did in those settings? Based on experience in these settings, what types of

> Knowing what people actually do in their daily lives helps preclude making inaccurate judgments about individual or group characteristics based on factors such as ethnicity, race, gender, socioeconomic status.

cultural models (beliefs, attitudes, values) have developed? How can the answers to these questions be used as resources in planning instruction? Knowing what people *actually do* in their daily lives helps preclude making inaccurate judgments about individual or group characteristics based on factors such as ethnicity, race, gender, socioeconomic status, and so forth. As many authors have noted (Gutierrez & Rogoff, 2003), it is extremely difficult to account for the variation among individuals within a group, especially in a way that would meaningfully help inform classroom practice. In contrast to the limited information labels based on ethnicity, race, and socioeconomic status provide regarding instructional practice, knowledge of these everyday cultural practices can be effectively and strategically used as instructional resources, as some authors have demonstrated (Gonzalez, Moll, & Amanti, 2005; Lee, C. D. 2005, 2007).

Which Theory Provides the Right Lens to Address Performance Problems?

In the example on reading instruction above, the reading intervention may not be wrong, but it may be an incomplete component of the whole set of issues needed to address the larger problem. What is called for is a framework that is able to fit diverse perspectives into one model so that they can be considered simultaneously, that is, a *comprehensive* or *multidimensional* approach. As one example, the National Research Council report on overrepresentation in special education (Donovan & Cross, 2002) described earlier in the chapter attempted to develop a contextual model with the myriad of specific factors related to student achievement (Figure 7.1).

One theoretical framework that intentionally connects learning, culture, and context as central concerns is sociohistorical or cultural-historical psychology. This approach emphasizes the processes of learning and development as a culturally, historically, and socially situated activity that can be understood only with reference to a given

> Knowledge of these everyday cultural practices can be effectively and strategically used as instructional resources.

cultural setting (Cole, 1996; Lave, 1996; Rogoff, 2003; see also Vygotsky, 1986; Wertsch, 1991). The terms sociocultural and sociohistorical are used here interchangeably. In general, they place primary emphasis on the interrelationship between individual, social, and cultural-historical factors in explaining learning and development. While these frameworks trace their roots back to Vygotsky's work, a great many authors have expanded upon his original ideas over the past half-century, in the United States as well as in European and Latin American countries. Extensive discussions are found in Cole, 1996; Cole, Engeström, & Vasquez, 1997; Forman, Minick, & Stone, 1993; Moll, 1990; Tharp & Gallimore, 1988; Wertsch, 1991, 1998. What is most important for our purposes here is that in matching school solutions to school problems, sociohistorical approaches start with the assumption that individual learning and development cannot be separated from the social context, and can only be completely understood in this larger perspective. Attending to this relationship needs to be a critical part of using a gap-analysis approach to solving school performance problems. The examples described previously about special education overrepresentation, and about language programs for English Learners illustrate how important this issue is.

Extensions of sociocultural theory by Rogoff (1995, 2003) are particularly germane to the current discussion. Rogoff has discussed learning and development as a function of one's transformation of participation in multiple interacting levels of influence, or *planes of development.* These planes of development include the individual, the interpersonal, and the cultural-institutional focus of analysis (see Figure 7.2). Factors at the individual level include cognitive, motivational, and other learning related characteristics that have typically been the central focus of educational research and intervention efforts designed to improve performance in schools. Specific targets of intervention, for example, include cognitive skills, learning strategies, metacognitive and executive factors, as well as motivation-related variables such as self-efficacy and attributions for failure and success. The significant and important work on learning and motivation in educational and cognitive psychology has largely focused on this level.

At the next level of this nested system is what is loosely called *interactional factors* that extend beyond the individual in isolation. These include interpersonal relationships, social interactions, and the social organizational and discourse features of the specific settings where people interact—whether it be the classroom, testing situation, or elsewhere. The level captures the important work by sociolinguists, educational anthropologists, developmental psychologists, and others who focus on interactional processes in a variety of educational, home, and community settings. In schools, these factors relate to the everyday interactions students, teachers, administrators, and parents, including how the features of the social context impact those interactions. As one example, there is good evidence that the social organization and classroom dynamics of classrooms have a strong influence on student motivation and learning (Au & Mason, 1981, 1983; Meece, Anderman, & Anderman, 2006).

Finally, the outermost level includes past and current institutional and community factors, particularly such things as home and family, community, and also the larger socio-political context that surrounds them. An example of the latter might be policy debates and conflict over issues like bilingual education, immigration, economic policies, distribution and allocation of economic resources, and so on, and the ways that these impact a particular family or community or school. It also focuses on factors such as current and past political, economic, and other types of power relationships among various groups. Particularly important is how these factors become embedded in the practices and values of social institutions like classrooms, schools, and districts, and how these are experienced by and impact individual groups and communities.

This plane of development is often overlooked in the behavioral sciences that guide so much educational practice, because it is not focused on individuals and is therefore seen as tangential to teaching and learning in schools. Yet these types of factors can have a significant impact on the educational experiences of students in one setting versus another.

From this multiple levels perspective, the causes of organizational performance issues and student achievement are neither within the child nor within the larger social and institutional system—rather, they are within the *interaction* of these multiple layers. That is, the *unit of analysis* is not any single level, but the combination of all considered as a unified whole. This is an important point related to the goal problem-solving in school settings, because if only a single level is considered, it is likely that other critical issues will remain unaddressed. It should be kept in mind that this framework is derived from basic established work in

> Causes of organizational performance issues and student achievement are neither within the child nor within the larger social and institutional system—rather, they are within the interaction of these multiple layers.

education, psychology, anthropology, and organizational theory. However, what *is* different and new is the simultaneous consideration of relevant factors in a comprehensive framework that facilitates a more complete approach to examining knowledge, motivational, and organizational gaps that diminish learning the achievement of school goals. This comprehensive perspective helps avoid some of the fragmentation, described earlier in the book that so often results in failure and bafflement by well-intentioned leaders.

AN EXAMPLE OF THE PLANES OF DEVELOPMENT IN PRACTICE

About a decade ago, a group of colleagues and I worked on a set of studies that were focused on reading and literacy as part of the research program of one of the national reading centers that existed at the time. The site where some of the work took place was in central Los Angeles, at an elementary school near the skid-row section of downtown. As with many urban schools, most of the students were poor, from homes where English was not the first language, and were either immigrants or children of immigrants, and academic achievement was near the bottom of the district. The school itself resembled something of a prison camp, with high fences, thick locks, and security guards, all designed to protect the school from the many dangers on the surrounding streets.

Many of the families worked in the garment factories, lived on the outskirts of downtown, and took the bus to work downtown. Many others lived in the shoddy downtown hotels, and a sizable number of students were homeless. This particular school, at the time of the study, had one of the largest numbers of homeless students in the country. Half of the 460 students were classified as homeless, and 92% were limited in English. Many students slept in shelters, a few in cars, others with relatives, and often did not know where they would be from one night to the next. Many if not most of the students and families were undocumented and lived in constant fear of deportation, a common occurrence when immigration authorities raided downtown factories.

At the time of the study, the English Only movement was gaining strength in California. Partly due to the efforts of a highly visible community activist, who adamantly opposed bilingual education, the school became a focal site for the debate on Proposition 227, the statewide effort to ban bilingual instruction. On a daily basis, there were protests, televised appearances, political rallies, and much public and media attention focused on the school. Eventually, the proposition passed and was enacted in to law. Emotions on the language issue, strongly associated with perceptions about the impact of immigration, ran high both at the school as well as in the larger public context.

It was during this same period that the reading wars (Allington, 2002) were coming to a head in the district, pitting the more constructivist whole language advocates against the more direct instruction basic skills advocates. In 1999, the district adopted a comprehensive reading plan to target low-achieving elementary schools, falling squarely on the basic skills side of the debate. The plan required all schools with 2nd- or 3rd-grade students scoring below the 50th percentile to adopt a research-based reading/language arts program, and the majority of elementary schools impacted chose to adopt the highly structured Open Court Reading program. The problem was that many teachers complained that it took away their freedom to adapt their curriculum to their students' needs, as fidelity to the program requirements became a paramount concern of the district. Moreover, the quick pacing of the program, and the fact that it was not designed for students who were not English speakers, made for a difficult time for some students and teachers, including several of those in our study. The principal (described in Chapter 5) was so burdened with bureaucratic reporting and administering all of the required initiatives and reforms that had been heaped on the school, that these did not permit her to function in the role of an instructional leader, compounding the problem.

As part of our work, we tried to capture a typical day for a student in the school. We produced the following schedule based on a composite of many students in the early elementary grades, which chronicled an average day:

- 5:00–6:00 a.m.—Wake up and go to babysitter on bus
- 6:00–7:00 a.m.—Go to school by bus or with babysitter
- 7:00–8:00 a.m.—Breakfast at home school
- 8:00–8:30 a.m.—Bussed to other campus for Latch Key Program (a school-based child-care program)
- 8:30–11:15 a.m.—Latch Key Program
- 11:15–11:30 a.m.—Bussed back to home school
- 11:30–12:10 p.m.—Lunch
- 12:10–3:30 p.m.—Instructional program

- 3:30–6:00 p.m.—Latch Key Program
- 6:00 p.m.—Latch Key Program closes, child rides bus home
- 7:00 p.m. or later—Arrive home

During visits to the families at home and in the community, we also noted how the families used literacy and reading in a variety of in-school and out-of-school contexts. Access to print materials was very limited for most families. To help address this situation, the school arranged for a weekly visit by a district bus that served as a mobile library. However, because of scarce resources, the policy was that each student could check out only two books. Many times these two books would already be read even before the van left the school. Unfortunately, no opportunity to trade these for new books would be available for another week. While some families used the downtown central library, the use of this resource was limited by time as well as economic factors. For example, the long work days limited the amount of time for library visits. One family who frequently used the library had to stop because fines for late books were beyond their means to pay.

By any stretch of the imagination, the circumstances of these families were exceedingly challenging, especially for young students. One has to wonder what it would take to achieve the goals outlined earlier in the book: the development of students who have acquired expertise, are engaged, can self-regulate, and who achieve on a wide variety of outcomes in and out of school.

It is true that a structured reading program might help a student in this situation build proficiency in basic reading skills, admittedly a strong need of most of the students we observed. However, given the multilevel framework outlined above, it is clear that this approach only addresses individual student cognitive factors. Where does a student in this situation develop an identity as a literate person who can accomplish complex tasks and activities with text? What are the opportunities to engage in meaningful conversation about a variety of text genres? How does a student like this develop a love of reading, an understanding of the ways that reading can be a way to discover the world? How does a student like this make sense of all of the sociopolitical issues that surround the school? On one of my visits to a classroom at the school, one of the teachers was trying to take advantage of the Proposition 227 controversy by having the students in the class examine both sides of this issue and engage in a debate. I recall a tiny 2nd-grade student asking

> Scaling up effective interventions is a good idea, but only when it makes sense for the local ecocultural settings, where it is to be used.

me, "Why are people against my language?" It was not a confrontational question, simply an effort by a young child to make sense of things that were not easily explainable, but that clearly formed a part of her learning environment.

This case may not be typical, but it does illustrate the fact that the sociocultural context matters. This is the case no matter how typical a school, classroom, or entire district might be, the argument is that the unit of analysis needs to go beyond the individual to include the multiple interacting planes of development that shape learning and development. The preceding chapters, therefore, should be considered in this light, rather than being applied in a mechanistic fashion. In theory, scaling up effective interventions is a good idea, but only when it makes sense for the local ecocultural settings, where it is to be used.

> No matter how typical a school, classroom, or entire district might be, the argument is that the unit of analysis needs to go beyond the individual to include the multiple interacting planes of development that shape learning and development.

CONCLUSION

It is hoped that the preceding chapters will provide new or more comprehensive ways of thinking about and addressing issues related to school performance and the achievement of important learning goals. Ultimately, our common goal as educators is the development of learners who are engaged and motivated, who can develop expertise in a variety of ways, who can self-regulate their own learning and motivation and adjust as needed, who understand that effort trumps IQ, and who perform to the best of their ability.

While the three-dimensional gap-analysis approach is systematic, it should not be thought of in rigid or inflexible terms, but rather as something to be used strategically according to the local need and circumstances, which can vary dramatically from one school to the next. Hopefully, it adds in a meaningful way to the array of tools that can be leveraged to help schools increase the opportunities for all students to learn, and to help create a more exciting environment for teachers and administrators to collaborate on their common goals.

Notes

Chapter 1

1. The terms *Hispanic* and *Latino* are often used interchangeably, and encompass those students often referred to as *English Learners* or *English Language Learners*. These labels encompass a range of students who vary in terms of socioeconomic status, language proficiency, immigration status, country of origin, and other important variables, and thus provide only very general information. Thus, caution needs to be exercised in making inferences about the specific characteristics of any individual or group based on these labels. In addition, it is important to recognize that there is not complete agreement in the literature regarding the most appropriate term. While the substance of this controversy will not be explored here, for purposes of expediency and consistency, the term *Latino* will be used unless otherwise noted.

Chapter 3

1. I cannot claim this toolkit as sole author, but am indebted to the students in my classes and to my colleagues at the University of Southern California (Richard Clark, Myron Dembo, Harry O'Neil, Giselle Ragusa, Ken Yates, and Kim Hirabayashi) who have all contributed to this over time.

Chapter 6

1. At the University of Southern California, a *thematic group* approach is used as the model for the dissertation project. Faculty and a group of students work on a common problem of practice. The format is meant to emulate the collaborative problem-solving work they will be expected to engage in within their professional work. In the work being described here, Dr. David Marsh and I collaborated on a gap-analysis project in two school districts with two thematic groups of students. Eighteen students were divided into collaborative work teams of three, and three of these teams worked in each district on different problems.

References

Agarao-Fernandez, E., & de Guzmán, A. B. (2006). Exploring the dimensionality of teacher professionalization. *Educational Research for Policy and Practice, 5*(3), 211–224.

Alexander, P. A. (2003). The development of expertise: The journey from acclimation to proficiency. *Educational Researcher, 32*(8), 10–14.

Alexander, P. A. (2006). *Psychology in learning and instruction.* Columbus, OH: Prentice Hall.

Alexander, P. A., Schallert, D. L., & Reynolds, R. E. (2009). What is learning anyway? A topographical perspective considered. *Educational Psychologist. 44*(3), 209–214.

Allington, R. L. (2002). *Big brother and the national reading curriculum: How ideology trumped evidence.* Portsmouth, NH: Heinemann.

Ames, C. (1992). Classrooms: Goals, structures, and student motivation. *Journal of Educational Psychology, 84*(3), 261–271.

Anderson, L. W., & Krathwohl, D. R., Airasian, P. W., Creikshank, K. A., Mayer, R. E., Pintrich, P. R., Raths, J., & Wittrick, M. C. (Eds.). (2001). *A taxonomy for learning, teaching, and assessing: A revision of Bloom's Taxonomy of educational objectives.* Allyn & Bacon. Boston, MA (Pearson Education Group).

Artiles, A. J., Rueda, R., Salazar, J., & Higareda, I. (2002). English-language learner representation in special education in California urban school districts. In D. J. Losen & G. Orfield (Eds.), *Racial inequality in special education* (pp. 265–284). Boston: Harvard Education Press.

Au, K. A. (2009). Negotiating the slippery slope: School change and literacy achievement. *Journal of Literacy Research, 37*(3), 267–288.

Au, K. H., & Mason, J. M. (1981). Social organizational factors in learning of reading: The balance of rights hypothesis. *Reading Research Quarterly, 17*(1), 115–152.

Au, K. H., & Mason, J. M. (1983). Cultural congruence in classroom participation structures: Achieving a balance of rights. *Discourse Processes, 6*(2), 145–167.

August, D., & Shanahan, T. (Eds.). (2006). *Developing literacy in second-language learners: Report of the National Literacy Panel on Language-Minority Children and Youth.* Mahwah, NJ: Lawrence Erlbaum Associates.

Azevedo, R., & Cromley, J. G. (2004). Does training on self-regulated learning facilitate students' learning with hypermedia? *Journal of Educational Psychology, 96*(3), 523–535.

Bandura, A. (1986). *Social foundations of thought and action.* Englewood Cliffs, NJ: Prentice Hall.

Bandura, A. (1997). *Self-efficacy: The exercise of control.* New York: Freeman.

Bandura, A. (2001). Social cognitive theory: An agentic perspective. *Annual Review of Psychology, 52,* 1–26.

Barrett, L. F., Tugade, M. M., & Engle, R. W. (2004). Individual differences in working memory capacity and dual-process theories of the mind. *Psychological Bulletin, 130*(4), 553–573. DOI: 10.1037/0033-2909.130.4.553

Bensimon, E. M., Polkinghorne, D. E., Bauman, G. L., & Vallejo, E. (2004). Doing research that makes a difference. *Journal of Higher Education, 75*(1), 104–126.

Berliner, D. C. (2002). Educational research: The hardest science of all. *Educational Researcher, 31*(8), 18–20.

Bernhardt, V. L. (2004 *Data analysis for continuous school improvement*). Larchmont, NY: Eye on Education.

Bloom, B. S. (Ed.), Englehard, M. D., Furst, E. J., Hill, W. H., & Krathwohl, D. R. (1956). *Taxonomy of educational objectives: Handbook I: Cognitive domain.* New York: David McKay.

Bolger, F., & Wright, G. (1992). Reliability and validity in expert judgment. In G. Wright & F. Bolger (Eds.), *Expertise and decision support* (pp. 47–76). New York: Plenum.

Boudett, K. P., City, E. A., & Murnane, R. J. (2007). *Data wise: A step-by-step guide to using assessment results to improve teaching and learning.* Cambridge, MA: Harvard University Press.

Boyles, D. (2005). *Schools or markets? Commercialism, privatization, and school-business partnerships.* Mahwah, NJ: Lawrence Erlbaum.

Bransford, J. D., Brown, A. L., & Cocking, R. R. (1999). *How people learn: Brain, mind, experience, and school.* Washington, DC: National Academy Press.

Brunner, C., Fasca, C., Heinze, J., Honey, M., Light, D., Mandinach, E., & Wexler, D. (2005). Linking data and learning: The Grow Network study. *Journal of Education for Students Placed At Risk, 10*(3), 241–267.

Butler, D., & Winne, P. H. (1995). Feedback and self-regulated learning: A theoretical synthesis. *Review of Educational Research, 65*(3), 245–281.

Carnegie Task Force on Teaching as a Profession. (1986). *A nation prepared: Teachers for the 21st century.* New York: Author.

Casanova, U. (2010). *¡Sí se puede!: Learning from a successful high school that beats the odds.* New York: Teachers College Press.

Chance, P. L. (2009). *Introduction to educational leadership and organizational behavior: Theory into practice.* Larchmont, NY: Eye on Education.

Charness, N., Krampe, R. T., & Mayr, U. (1996). The role of practice and coaching in entrepreneurial skill domains: An international comparison of life-span chess skill acquisition. In K. A. Ericsson (Ed.), *The road to excellence: The acquisition of expert performance in the arts and sciences, sports, and games* (pp. 51–80). Mahwah, NJ: Erlbaum.

Chi, M. T. H., Glaser, R., & Rees, E. (1982). Expertise in problem solving. In R. S. Sternberg (Ed.), *Advances in the psychology of human intelligence* (pp. 7–75). Hillsdale, NJ: Erlbaum.

Clark, R. E. (2004). See the forest, tend the trees: Analyzing and solving accountability problems. *Urban Ed: The Magazine of the Rossier School of Education* (pp. 20–22). Los Angeles: University of Southern California.

Clark, R. E. (2005). Research-tested team motivation strategies. *Performance Improvement, 44*(1), 13–16.

Clark, R. E. (2006). Not knowing what we don't know: Reframing the importance of automated knowledge for educational research. In G. Clarebout & J. Elen (Eds.), *Avoiding simplicity, confronting complexity: Advances in studying and designing (computer based) powerful learning environments* (pp. 3-15). Rótterdam, The Netherlands: Sense Publishers.

Clark, R. E. (2008). Resistance to change: Unconscious knowledge and the challenge of unlearning. In D. C. Berliner, & H. Kupermintz (Eds.), *Changing institutions, environments, and people* (pp. –). Mahwah, NJ: Lawrence Erlbaum Associates.

Clark, R. E., & Estes, F. (2008). *Turning research into results: A guide to selecting the right performance solutions.* Atlanta: CEP Press.

Cochran-Smith, M., & Lytle, S. L. (2006). Troubling images of teaching in No Child Left Behind. *Harvard Educational Review, 76*(4), 668–697.

Cole, M. (1985). The zone of proximal development: Where culture and cognition create each other. In J. V. Wertsch (Ed.), *Culture, communication, and cognition: Vygotskian perspectives* (pp. 146–161). Cambridge, UK: Cambridge University Press.

Cole, M. (1996). *Cultural psychology: A once and future discipline.* Cambridge, MA: Harvard University Press.

Cole, M., Engeström, Y., & Vasquez, O. (1997). *Mind, culture, and activity: Seminal papers from the Laboratory of Comparative Human Cognition.* New York: Cambridge University Press.

Comber, M. K. (2005). *The effects of civic education on civic skills* [CIRCLE fact sheet]. Medford, MA: The Center for Information and Research on Civic Learning and Engagement. Retrieved January 12, 2011, from http://www.civicyouth.org/fact-sheet-the-effects-of-civic-education-on-civic-skills/

Cox, K., & Guthrie, J. T. (2001). Motivational and cognitive contributions to students' amount of reading. *Contemporary Educational Psychology, 26*(1), 116–131.

Crawford, J. (2004). *Educating English learners: Language diversity in the classroom.* Los Angeles: Bilingual Education Services.

Cummins, J. (1998). Immersion education for the millennium: What have we learned from 30 years of research on second language immersion? In M. R. Childs & R. M. Bostwick (Eds.), *Learning through two languages: Research and practice* (pp. 34–47). Second Katoh Gakuen International Symposium on Immersion and Bilingual Education, Katoh Gakuen, Japan.

Darling-Hammond, L., & Sykes, G. (2003). Meeting the "highly qualified teacher" challenge. *Teacher Education and Practice, 16*(4), 331–354.

Datnow, A., Hubbard, L., & Mehan, H. (2002). *Extending educational reform: From one school to many.* London: Routledge/Falmer Press.

Datnow, A., Lasky, S., Stringfield, S., & Teddlie, C. (2005). *Integrating educational systems for successful reform in diverse contexts.* Cambridge, MA: Cambridge University Press.

Davila, A., & Mora, M. T. (2007) *Civic engagement and high school academic progress: An analysis using NELS data* (CIRCLE Working Paper No. 52). Medford, MA: The Center for Information and Research on Civic Learning and Engagement. Retrieved January 12, 2011, from http://www.civicyouth.org/PopUps/WorkingPapers/WP52Mora.pdf

Deci, E. L. & Ryan, R. M. (1985). *Intrinsic motivation and self-determination in human behavior.* New York: Plenum Press.

Dobb, F. (2004). *Essential elements of effective science instruction for English learners.* Los Angeles: California Science Project.

Donovan, S., & Cross, C. (Eds.). (2002). *Minority students in special and gifted education.* Washington, DC: National Academy Press.

Echevarria, J., Vogt, M. E., & Short, D. (2008). *Making content comprehensible to English learners: The SIOP model* (3rd ed.). Boston: Pearson/Allyn & Bacon.

Eisenhart, M., & Towne, L. (2003). Contestation and change in national policy on "scientifically based" education research. *Educational Researcher, 32*(7), 31–38.

Elliot, A. J. (2006). The hierarchical model of approach-avoidance motivation. *Motivation and Emotion, 30*(2), 111–116.

Elmore, R. F. (2003). *Doing the right thing, knowing the right thing to do: School improvement and performance-based accountability.* Washington, DC: National Governors Association Center for Best Practices.

Engeström, Y., Miettinen, R., & Punamäki, R. (1999). *Perspectives on activity theory.* New York: Cambridge University Press.

Epstein, J. (1989). Family structures and student motivation: A developmental perspective. In C. Ames & R. Ames (Eds.), *Research on motivation in education* (Vol. 3, pp. 259–295). San Diego, CA: Academic Press.

Erickson, F. (2004). Culture in society and in educational practices. In J. A. Banks & C. A. M. Banks (Eds.), *Handbook of research on multicultural education* (2nd ed., pp. 33–58). San Francisco: Jossey-Bass.

Ericsson, K. A. (1998). The scientific study of expert levels of performance: General implications for optimal learning and creativity. *High Ability Studies, 9*(1), 75–100.

Ericsson, K. A., & Charness, N. (1994). Expert performance: Its structure and acquisition. *American Psychologist, 49*(8), 725–747.

Ericsson, K. A., Krampe, R. T., & Tesch-Römer, C. (1993). The role of deliberate practice in the acquisition of expert performance. *Psychological Review, 100*(3), 363–406.

Ericsson, K. A., & Lehmann, A. C. (1996). Expert and exceptional performance: Evidence on Expert and exceptional performance: Evidence on maximal adaptations on task constraints maximal adaptations on task constraints. *Annual Review of Psychology, 47*, 273–305.

Feldon, D. F. (2007). Implications of research on expertise for curriculum and pedagogy. *Educational Psychology Review, 19*(2), 91–110.

Feldon, D. F. (2008). Expertise. In E. Anderman & L. Anderman (Eds.), *Psychology of classroom learning: An encyclopedia* (pp. –). Detroit, MI: Macmillan Reference USA.

Ferrance, E. (2000). *Action research*. Providence, RI: Northeast and Islands Regional Laboratory at Brown University.

Forman, E. A., Minick, N., & Stone, C. A. (1993). *Contexts for learning: Sociocultural dynamics in children's development*. New York: Oxford University Press.

Fredericks, J., Blumenfeld, P., & Paris, A. (2004). School engagement: Potential of the concept, state of the evidence. *Review of Educational Research, 74*(1), 59–109.

Fry, R. (2007). *How far behind in math and reading are English language learners?* Washington, DC: Pew Hispanic Center.

Fuchs, D., Mock, D., Morgan, P. L., & Young, C. L. (2003). Responsiveness-to-intervention: Definitions, evidence, and implications for the learning disabilities construct. *Learning Disabilities Research & Practice, 18* (3), 204–219.

Furrer, C., & Skinner, E. (2003). Sense of relatedness as a factor in children's academic engagement and performance. *Journal of Educational Psychology, 95*(1), 148–162.

Gallimore, R., & Goldenberg, C. (2001). Analyzing cultural models and settings to connect minority achievement and school improvement research. *Educational Psychologist, 36*(1), 45–56.

Gándara, P. (2005). *Latino achievement: Identifying models that foster success*. Storrs, CT: National Center for the Gifted and Talented, University of Connecticut.

Gándara, P., & Gomez, M. C. (2009. Language policy in education. In B. Schneider, G. Sykes, & D. Plank (Eds.), *Handbook of Education Policy Research*. (pp. 581–595). Washington, DC: American Educational Research Association.

Gándara, P., Rumberger, R., Maxwell-Jolly, J., & Callahan, R. (2003). English learners in California schools: Unequal resources, unequal outcomes. *Education Policy Analysis Archives, 11*(36). Retrieved on February 7, 2011 from http://epaa.asu.edu/epaa/v11n36/

Garcia, E. (2005). *Teaching and learning in two languages: Bilingualism and schooling in the United States.* New York: Teachers College Press.

Genesee, F. (1985). Second language learning through immersion: A review of U.S. programs. *Review of Educational Research, 55*(4), 541–561.

Genesee, F., & Lindholm-Leary, K. (2007). Dual language education in Canada and the United States. In J. Cummins & N. Hornberger (Eds.), *Encyclopedia of language and education* (2nd ed., pp. 253–266). New York: Springer.

Genesee, F., Lindholm-Leary, K., Saunders, W., & Christian, D. (2005). English language learners in U.S. schools: An overview of research findings. *Journal of Education for Students at Risk, 10*(4), 363–385.

Genesee, F., Lindholm-Leary, K., Saunders, W., & Christian, D. (2006). *Educating English language learners: A synthesis of research evidence.* New York: Cambridge University Press.

Glatthorn, A. A., & Jailall, J. M. (2009). *The principal as curriculum leader: Shaping what is taught and tested.* Thousand Oaks, CA: Corwin Press.

Goldenberg, C. (2008). Teaching English language learners: What the research does—and does not—say. *American Education, 32*(2), 8–44.

González, N., Moll, L., & Amanti, C. (2004). Introduction: Theorizing practices. In N. González, L. Moll, & C. Amanti (Eds.), *Funds of knowledge: Theorizing practices in households, communities, and classrooms* (pp. 1–28). Mahwah, NJ: Lawrence Erlbaum Associates.

González, N., Moll, L., & Amanti, C. (2005). *Funds of knowledge: Theorizing practices in households, communities, and classrooms.* Mahwah, NJ: Lawrence Erlbaum Associates.

Graham, S., & Hudley, C. (2007). Race and ethnicity in the study of motivation and competence. In A. J. Elliot & C. S. Dweck (Eds.), *Handbook of competence and motivation* (pp. 392–413). New York: Guilford Press.

Gredler, M. E. (2009). *Learning and instruction: Theory into practice* (6th ed.). New York: Prentice Hall.

Guthrie, J. T., & Wigfield, A. (2000). Engagement and motivation in reading. In M. Kamil, R. Barr, P. Mosenthal & D. Pearson (Eds.), *Handbook of reading research II, I* (pp. 403–422). New York: Longman.

Gutierrez, K. D., & Rogoff, B. (2003). Cultural ways of learning: Individual styles or repertoires of practice. *Educational Researcher, 32*(5), 19–25.

Halverson, R., Grigg, J., Prichett, R., & Thomas, C. (2007). The new instructional leadership: Creating data-driven instructional systems in schools. *Journal of School Leadership, 17*(2), 158–193.

Hamilton, L., Halverson, R., Jackson, S., Mandinach, E., Supovitz, J., & Wayman, J. (2009). *Using student achievement data to support instructional decision making* (NCEE 2009-4067). Washington, DC: National Center for Education Evaluation and Regional Assistance, Institute of Education Sciences, U.S. Department of Education.

Harry, B., & Klinger, J. K. (2006). *Why are so many minority students in special education? Understanding race and disability in schools.* New York: Teachers College Press.

Harry, B., Klinger, J. K., & Cramer, E. (2007). *Case studies in the social construction of disability: Minority students in special education.* New York: Teachers College Press.

Hassel, B., Hassel, E., & Rhim, L. M. (2007). Overview of restructuring. In H. J. Walberg (Ed.), *Handbook on restructuring and substantial school improvement* (pp. 9–22). Lincoln, IL: Center on Innovation and Improvement. Retrieved January 12, 2011, from http://www.centerii.org/survey/downloads/Restructuring%20Handbook.pdf

Hatano, G., & Inagaki, K. (2000, April). Practice makes a difference: Design principles for adaptive expertise. Presentation at the annual meeting of the American Educational Research Association, New Orleans.

Hatano, G., & Oura, Y. (2003). Commentary: Reconceptualizing school learning using insight from expertise research. *Educational Researcher, 32*(8), 26–29.

Heller, K. A., Holtzman, W. H., & Messick, S. (Eds.). (1982). *Placing children in special education: A strategy for equity.* Washington, DC: National Academy Press.

Herrnstein, R. J., & Murray, C. (1994). *The bell curve: Intelligence and class structure in American life.* New York: Free Press Paperbacks.

Holcomb, E. (1999). *Getting excited about data: How to combine people, passion, and proof.* Thousand Oaks, CA: Corwin Press.

Horn, R. A. (2007). Curriculum, instruction, and assessment in a reconceptualized educational environment. In J. K. Kincheloe & R. A. Horn (Eds.), *The Praeger handbook of education and psychology* (pp. 824–835). Portsmouth, NH: Greenwood Publishing Group.

Hudley, C., & Daoud, A. M. (2007). High school students' engagement in school: Understanding the relationship between school context and student expectations. In F. Salili & F. Hoosain (Eds.), *Culture, motivation, and learning: A multicultural perspective* (pp. 365–390). Charlotte, NC: Information Age Publishing.

Hudley, C., Graham, S., & Taylor, A. (2007). Reducing aggressive behavior and increasing motivation in school: The evolution of an intervention to strengthen school adjustment. *Educational Psychologist, 42*(4), 251–260.

Imants, J. (2003). Two basic mechanisms for organizational learning in schools. *European Journal of Teacher Education, 26*(3), 293–311.

Immordino-Yang, M. H. & Sylvan, L. (2010). Admiration for virtue: Neuroscientific perspectives on a motivating emotion. *Contemporary Educational Psychology, 35*(2), 110–115.

Individuals with Disabilities Education Improvement Act of 2004, Pub. L. 108–466.

Jimerson, S. R., Campos, E., & Greif, J. L. (2003). Toward an understanding of definitions and measures of school engagement and related terms. *California School Psychologist, 8*, 7–27.

Johnson, R. K., & Swain, M. (1997). *Immersion education: International perspectives.* Cambridge, UK: Cambridge University Press.

Johnson, R. S. (2002). *Using data to close the achievement gap: How to measure equity in our schools.* Thousand Oaks, CA: Corwin Press.

Kahne, J., & Middaugh, E. (2008). *Democracy for some: The civic opportunity gap in high school* [CIRCLE Working Paper No. 59]. Medford, MA: The Center for Information and Research on Civic Learning and Engagement. Retrieved January 12, 2011, from http://www.civicyouth.org/PopUps/WorkingPapers/WP59Kahne.pdf

Kenny, M. E., Blustein, D. L., Chaves, A., Grossman, J. M., & Gallagher, L. A. (2003). The role of perceived barriers and relational support in the educational and vocational lives of urban high school students. *Journal of Counseling Psychology, 50*(2), 142–155.

Kezar, A. (2005). *Organizational learning in higher education.* San Francisco: Jossey-Bass.

Kezar, A. J., Chambers, T. C. & Burkhardt, J. C. (2005). *Higher education for the public good: Emerging voices from a national movement.* San Francisco: Jossey-Bass.

Kirkpatrick, D. L. (2006). Seven keys to unlock the four levels of evaluation. *Performance Improvement, 45*(7), 5–8.

Kirpatrick, D. L, & Kirpatrick, J. D. (2006). *Evaluating training programs: The four levels* (3rd ed.). San Francisco: Berrett-Koehler Publishers.

Kirsch, I., de Jong, J., LaFontaine, D., McQueen, J., Mendelovits, J., & Monseur, C. (2002). *Reading for change: Performance and engagement across countries.* Paris: Organisation for Economic Co-operation and Development.

Klinger, J. K., & Edwards, P. (2006). Cultural considerations with response to intervention models. *Reading Research Quarterly, 41,* 108–117.

Kozulin, A., Gindis, B., Ageyez, V. S., & Miller, S. M. (2003). *Vygotsky's educational theory in cultural context.* New York: Cambridge University Press.

Krathwohl, D. R. (2002). A revision of Bloom's taxonomy: An overview. *Theory into Practice, 41*(4), 212–218.

Lankford, H. Loeb, S. & Wyckoff, J. (2002). Teacher sorting and the plight of urban schools: A descriptive analysis. *Education Evaluation and Policy Analysis, 24*(1), 37–62.

Lave, J. (1996). Teaching, as learning in practice. *Mind, Culture, and Activity, 3*(3)149–164.

Lee, C. D. (2005). Taking culture into account: Intervention research based on current views of cognition and learning. In J. King (Ed.), *Black education: A transformative research and action agenda for the new century* (pp. 43–44). Mahwah, NJ: Lawrence Erlbaum; Washington, DC: American Educational Research Association.

Lee, C. D. (2007). *Culture, literacy, and learning: Taking bloom in the midst of the whirlwind.* New York: Teachers College Press.

Lee, O. (2005). Science education with English language learners: Synthesis and research agenda. *Review of Educational Research, 75*(4), 491–530.

Levin, H. (2001). *Privatizing education: Can the school marketplace deliver freedom of choice, efficiency, equity, and social cohesion?* Boulder, CO: Westview Press.

Ley, K., & Young, D. B. (2001). Instructional principles for self-regulation. *Educational Technology, Research, and Development, 49*(2), 93–103.

Linn, R. L. (2000). Assessments and accountability. *Educational Researcher, 29*(2), 4–16.

Linn, R. L. (2003). Accountability: Responsibility and reasonable expectations. *Educational Researcher, 32*(7), 3–13.

Locke, E. A., & Latham, G. P. (1990). *A theory of goal setting and task performance.* Englewood Cliffs, NJ: Prentice Hall.

Locke, E. A., & Latham, G. P. (2002). Building a practically useful theory of goal setting and task motivation: A 35-year odyssey. *American Psychologist, 57*(9), 705–717.

Longo, N. V. (2007). *Why community matters: Connecting education with civic life.* Albany: State University of New York Press.

Love, N. (2002). *Using data/getting results: A practical guide for school improvement in mathematics and science.* Norwood, MA: Christopher-Gordon.

Lundberg, C. A., & Schreiner, L. A. (2004). Quality and frequency of faculty-student interaction as predictors of learning: An analysis by student race/ethnicity. *Journal of College Student Development, 45*(5), 549–565.

Lutkus, A., Grigg, W., & Donahue, P. (2007). *The nation's report card: Trial urban district assessment reading 2007* [NCES 2008-455]. Washington, DC: National Center for Education Statistics, Institute of Education Sciences, U.S. Department of Education.

Mandinach, E. B., & Honey, M. (2008). *Data driven school improvement: Linking data and learning.* New York: Teachers College Press.

Marsh, D. D., Dembo, M., Gallagher, K. S., & Stowe, K. (2010). Examining the capstone experience in a cutting edge Ed.D. program. In J. M. Gaetane & A. H. Normore (Eds.), *Educational leadership preparation: Innovation and interdisciplinary approaches to the Ed.D. and graduate education.* (pp. 203–236). New York: Palgrave Macmillan.

Mayer, R. E. (2008). *Learning and instruction.* Upper Saddle River, NJ: Pearson Merrill Prentice Hall.

Mayer, R. E. (2011). *Applying the science of learning.* Boston: Pearson.

McInerney, D. M. & Van Etten, S. (Eds.) (2001). *Research on sociocultural influences on motivation and learning, Volume 1.* Greenwich, CT: Information Age Publishing.

McInerney, D., & Van Etten, S. (2002). *Research on sociocultural influences on motivation and learning* (Vol. 2). Charlotte, NC: Information Age Publishing.

McInerney, D., & Van Etten, S. (2004). *Big theories revisited.* Greenwich, CT: Information Age Publishing.

Meece, J. L., Anderman, E. M., & Anderman, L. H. (2006). Classroom goal structure, student motivation, and academic achievement. *Annual Review of Psychology, 57,* 487–503.

Meece, J. L., Blumenfeld, P., & Hoyle, R. (1988). Students' goal orientations and cognitive engagement in classroom activities. *Journal of Educational Psychology, 80*(4), 514–523.

Meltzoff, A. N., Kuhl, P. K. Movellan, J., & Sejnowski, T. J. (2009). Foundations for a new science of learning. *Science, 325*(5938), 284–288.

Mercer, J. R. (1973). *Labeling the mentally retarded.* Berkeley & Los Angeles: University of California Press.

Merton, R. K. (1968). The Matthew effect in science. *Science, 159*(3810), 56–63.

Mills, G. E. (2003). *Action research: A guide for the teacher researcher.* Upper Saddle River, NJ: Merrill/Prentice Hall.

Moll, L. C. (1990). *Vygotsky and education.* New York: Cambridge University Press.

Monzo, L., & Rueda, R. (2000). Constructing achievement orientations toward literacy: An analysis of sociocultural activity in Latino home and community contexts. *National Reading Conference Yearbook, 49,* 405–420.

Monzo, L., & Rueda, R. (2009). Passing as English fluent: Latino immigrant children masking language proficiency. *Anthropology & Education Quarterly, 40*(1), 20–40.

Moreno, R. (2010). *Educational psychology.* Hoboken, NJ: John Wiley & Sons.

Moss, P. A., Girard, B. J., & Haniford, L. C. (2006). Validity in educational assessment. In J. Green & A. Luke (Eds.), *Rethinking learning: What counts as learning and what learning counts (Review of research in education,* Vol. 30, pp. 109–162). Washington, DC: American Educational Research Association.

National Research Council. (2002). *Scientific research in education* (R. J. Shavelson & L. Towne, Eds.). Washington, DC: Committee on Scientific Principles for Education Research, Center for Education, Division of Behavioral and Social Sciences and Education, National Academy Press.

National Research Council. (2004). *Engaging schools: Fostering high school students' motivation to learn.* Washington, DC: Committee on Increasing High School Students' Engagement and Motivation to Learn, National Academies Press.

National Research Council. (2008). *Common standards for K–12 education? Considering the evidence.* Washington, DC: National Academies Press.

Noffke, S., & Somekh, B. (Eds.). (2009). *The SAGE handbook of educational action research.* London: SAGE Publications.

Ormrod, J. E. (2010). *Educational psychology: Developing learners* (7th ed.). Upper Saddle River: NJ: Prentice Hall.

Pajares, F. (2007). Culturalizing educational psychology. In F. Salili & F. Hoosain (Eds.), *Culture, motivation, and learning: A multicultural perspective* (pp. 19–42). Charlotte, NC: Information Age Publishing.

Pekrun, R. (2007). The control-value theory of achievement emotions: An integrative approach to emotions in education. In R. Schulze & R. D. Roberts (Eds.), *Emotional intelligence: An international handbook* (pp. 13–36). Cambridge, MA: Hogrefe & Huber Publishers.

Pintrich, P. R. (2003). A motivational science perspective on the role of student motivation in learning and teaching contexts. *Journal of Educational Psychology, 95*(4), 667–686.

Pintrich, P. R., Schunk, D. H., & Meece, J. L. (2008). *Motivation in education: Theory, research, and applications* (3rd ed.). Upper Saddle River, NJ: Merrill.

Planty, M., Hussar, W., Snyder, T., Provasnik, S., Kena, G., Dinkes, R., Kewal Ramani, A., & Kemp, J. (2008). *The condition of education 2008* [NCES 2008-031]. Washington, DC: National Center for Education Statistics, Institute of Education Sciences, U.S. Department of Education.

Plato Learning. (2003). *Choosing and using learning technology: Making evidence-based decisions*. Bloomington, MN: Author.

Rogoff, B. (1995). Observing sociocultural activity on three planes: Participatory appropriation, guided participation, and apprenticeship. In J. V. Wertsch, P. del Rio, & A. Alvarez (Eds.), *Sociocultural studies of mind* (pp. 139–164). Cambridge: Cambridge University Press.

Rogoff, B. (2003). *The cultural nature of human development*. New York: Cambridge University Press.

Rueda, R., & Dembo, M. (2006). Rethinking learning and motivation in urban schools. In J. L. Kincheloe, K. Hayes, K. Rose, & P. M. Anderson (Eds.), *The Praeger handbook of urban education, Vol. 2* (pp. 217–226). Westport, CT: Greenwood Publishing Group.

Salili, F., & Hoosain, F. (2007). *Culture, motivation, and learning: A multicultural perspective*. Charlotte, NC: Information Age Publishing.

Saunders, W. M., Goldenberg, C. N., & Gallimore, R. (2009). Increasing achievement by focusing grade-level teams on improving classroom learning: A prospective, quasi-experimental study of Title I schools. *American Educational Research Journal, 46*(4), 1006–1033.

Schein, E. H. (2004a). The concept of organizational culture: Why bother? In E. H. Schein (Ed.), *Organizational culture and leadership* (3rd ed., pp. 3–23). San Francisco: Jossey-Bass.

Schein, E. H. (2004b). *Organizational culture and leadership* (3rd ed.). San Francisco: Jossey-Bass.

Schoenfeld, A. H. (2006). What doesn't work: The challenge and failure of the What Works Clearinghouse to conduct meaningful reviews of studies of mathematics curricula. *Educational Researcher, 35*(2), 13–21.

Schunk, D. H., & Pajares, F. (2005). Competence perceptions and academic functioning. In A. J. Elliot & C. S. Dweck (Eds.), *Handbook of competence and motivation* (pp. 85–104). New York: Guilford Press.

Schunk, D. H., Pintrich, P. R., & Meece, J. L. (2009). *Motivation in education: Theory, research, and application.* Upper Saddle River, NJ: Pearson/Merrill Prentice Hall.

Schyns, B., & Hansbrough, T. (2010). *When leadership goes wrong: Destructive leadership, mistakes, and ethical failures.* Charlotte, NC: Information Age Press.

Shulman, L. S., Golde, C. M., Bueschel, A. C., & Garabedian, K. J. (2006). Reclaiming education's doctorates: A critique and a proposal. *Educational Researcher, 35*(3), 25–32.

Skinner, E., Furrer, C., Marchand, G., & Kindermann, T. (2008). Engagement and disaffectation in the classroom: Part of a larger motivational dynamic? *Journal of Educational Psychology, 100*(4), 765–781.

Skinner, E., Zimmer-Gembeck, M. & Connell, J. (1998). Individual differences and the development of perceived control. *Monographs of the Society for Research in Child Development, 63*(2–3, Serial No. 254).

Slavin, R. E. (2009). *Educational psychology: Theory into practice* (9th ed.). Upper Saddle River, NJ: Pearson Education, Inc.

Sloboda, J. A., Davidson, J. W., Howe, M. J. A., & Moore, D. G. (1996). The role of practice in the development of performing musicians. *British Journal of Psychology, 87*, 287–309.

Snow, C. E., & Biancarosa, G. (2003). *Adolescent literacy and the achievement gap: What do we know and where do we go from here?* (p. 7). New York: Carnegie Corporation.

Snyder, T.D., Tan, A.G., & Hoffman, C.M. (2004). *Digest of Education Statistics 2003,*(NCES 2005–025). U.S. Department of Education, National Center for Education Statistics. Washington, DC: Government Printing Office.

Starkes, J. L., Deakin, J. M., Allard, F., Hodges, N. J., & Hayes, A. Deliberate practice in sports: What is it anyway? In K. A. Ericsson (Ed.), *The road to excellence: The acquisition of expert performance in the arts and sciences, sports, and games* (pp. 81–106). Mahwah, NJ: Erlbaum.

Starkes, J. L., Deakin, J., Allard, F., Hodges, N. J., & Hayes, A. (1996). *Deliberate practice in education* (Vol. 2, pp. 217–226). Westport, CT: Greenwood Press.

Stecher, B. M., McCaffrey, D. F. & Bugliari, D. (2003, November 10). The relationship between exposure to class size reduction and student achievement in California. *Education Policy Analysis Archives, 11*(40). Retrieved March 25, 2009 from http://epaa.asu.edu/epaa/v11n40/

Steele, J. L., Murnane, R. J. & Willett, J. B. (2009). *Do financial incentives help low-performing schools attract and keep academically talented teachers? Evidence from California* [NBER Working Paper No. w14780]. Available at http://ssrn.com/abstract=1359476

Stevenson, H. J. (2008). To adapt or survive: Teachers' informal collaboration and view of mandated curricula. *Issues in Teacher Education, 17*(1), 75–95.

Swain, M. (2000). French immersion research in Canada: Recent contributions to SLA and applied linguistics. *Annual Review of Applied Linguistics, 20*, 199–212.

Thacker, T., Bell, J. S., & Schargel, F. P. (2009). *Creating school cultures that embrace learning: What successful leaders do.* Larchmont, NY: Eye on Education.

Tharp, R. G., & Gallimore, R. (1988). *Rousing minds to life: Teaching, learning, and schooling in social context.* Cambridge: Cambridge University Press.

The Oxford New Revised Standard Version Anglicized Cross-Reference Edition. (1995). New York: Oxford University Press.

Torney-Purta, J., & Wilkenfeld, B. S. (2009). *Paths to 21st century competencies through civic education classrooms: An analysis of survey results from ninth-graders.* Chicago, IL: American Bar Association Division for Public Education.

U.S. Department of Education. (2002). *Improving performance: A five step process.* Washington, DC: Division of Vocational and Technical Information.

U.S. Department of Education, National Center for Education Statistics. (2006). *Public elementary and secondary students, staff, schools, and school districts: School year 2003–04* [NCES 2006–307]. Washington, DC: Author.

U.S. Department of Education, Office of Innovation and Improvement. (2006). *Charter high schools: Closing the achievement gap.* Washington, DC: Author.

Valencia, R. R. (2010). *Dismantling contemporary deficit thinking: Educational thought and practice.* New York: Routledge.

Valenzuela, A. (1999). *Subtractive schooling: US-Mexican youth and the politics of caring.* New York: State University of New York Press.

Vernez, G., Karam, R., Mariano, L. & DeMartini, C. (2006) *Evaluating comprehensive school reform models at scale: A focus on implementation.* Santa Monica, CA: Rand Corporation.

Vygotsky, L. S. (1986). *Thought and language* (A. Kozulin, Ed.). Cambridge, MA: MIT Press.

Waitoller, F. R., Artiles, A. J., & Cheney, D. (2010). The miners' canary: A review of overrepresentation research and explanations. *Journal of Special Education, 44*(1), 29–49.

Wentzel, K. R. (2000). What is it that I'm trying to achieve? Classroom goals from an achievement perspective. *Contemporary Educational Psychology, 25,* 105–115.

Wentzel, K. R., & Wigfield, A. (2009). *Handbook of motivation at school.* New York: Routledge.

Wertsch, J. V. (1991). *Voices of the mind: A sociocultural approach to mediated action.* Cambridge, MA: Harvard University Press.

Wertsch, J. V. (1998). *Mind as action.* New York: Oxford University Press.

Wiener, B. (2005). Motivation from an attribution perspective and the social psychology of perceived competence. In A. Elliot & C. Dweck (Eds.), *Handbook of competence and motivation* (pp. 73–84). New York: Guilford Press.

Wigfield, A., & Eccles, J. S. (2000). Expectancy value theory of motivation. *Contemporary Educational Psychology, 25,* 68–81. DOI: 10.1006/ceps.1999.1015.

Wigfield, A., & Eccles, J. S. (2002). The development of competence beliefs, expectancies for success, and achievement values from childhood through adolescence. In A. Wigfield & J. S. Eccles (Eds.), *Development of achievement motivation* (pp. 91–120). San Diego: Academic Press.

Zepeda, S. (2007). *The principal as instructional leader: A handbook for supervisors.* Larchmont, NY: Eye on Education.

Zimmerman, B. J. (2000). Attaining self-regulation: A social-cognitive perspective. In M. Boekaerts, P. R. Pintrich, & M. Zeidner (Eds.), *Handbook of self-regulation* (pp. 13–39). San Diego: Academic Press.

Zimmerman, B. J. (2008). Investigating self-regulation and motivation: Historical background, methodological developments, and future prospects. *American Educational Research Journal, 45*(1), 166–183.

Zimmerman, B. J., & Cleary, T. J. (2009). Motives to self-regulate learning: A social cognitive account. In K. R. Wentzel & A. Wigfield (Eds.), *Handbook of motivation at school* (pp. 247–264). New York: Routledge.

Zimmerman, B. J., & Martinez-Pons, M. (1990). Student differences in self-regulated learning: Relating grade, sex, and giftedness to self-efficacy and strategy use. *Journal of Educational Psychology, 82*(1), 51–59.

Zimmerman, B. J., & Schunk, D. H. (Eds.). (2001). *Self-regulated learning and academic achievement: Theory, research and practice.* New York: Springer-Verlag.

Index

About the Author

Robert Rueda is the Stephen H. Crocker Professor of Education at the Rossier School of Education at the University of Southern California, where he teaches in the area of Psychology in Education. He also has a joint appointment in the Psychology Department. He completed his doctoral work at the University of California at Los Angeles in Educational Psychology and completed a postdoctoral fellowship at the Laboratory of Comparative Human Cognition at the University of California, San Diego in cross-cultural psychology. His research has centered on the sociocultural basis of motivation, learning, and instruction, with a focus reading and literacy in English learners, and students in at-risk conditions, and he teaches courses in learning and motivation. He served as a panel member on the National Academy of Science Report on the Overrepresentation of Minority Students in Special Education, and also served as a member of the National Literacy Panel (SRI International and Center for Applied Linguistics) looking at issues in early reading with English language learners. He is a fellow of the American Psychological Association and of the American Educational Research Association, and is also a member of the International Society for Cultural Research and Activity Theory, the Council for Exceptional Children (Mental Retardation Division; Learning Disabilities Division; Division for Culturally and Linguistically Diverse Exceptional Learners), the American Anthropological Association (Council on Anthropology and Education), the International Reading Association, the California Reading Association, and the National Reading Conference. He recently served as the associate editor of the *American Educational Research Journal,* and currently serves on the editorial boards of several educational journals. He chairs the committee which oversees the Ed.D. Doctoral Program in the Rossier School.